ZERO BELLY COOKBOOK

Delicious Meals to Boost Metabolism, Burn Fat, and Transform Your Body

Sarah White

Copyright Material ©2023

All Rights Reserved

No part of this book may be used or transmitted in any form or by any means without the proper written consent of the publisher and copyright owner, except for brief quotations used in a review. This book should not be considered a substitute for medical, legal, or other professional advice.

TABLE OF CONTENTS

TABLE OF CONTENTS..3
INTRODUCTION..7
BREAKFASTS..9
1. Zero-Belly Pancakes and Syrup..10
2. Bacon Avocado Breakfast Muffins....................................12
3. Orange Cinnamon Scones..15
4. Red Pepper, Mozzarella and Bacon Frittata....................18
5. Cheese and Sausage Pies..21
6. Breakfast Quiche..23
7. Chicharrones con Huevos (Pork Rind and Eggs)............25
8. Raspberry & Cacao Breakfast Bowl..................................27
9. Anaheim pepper Gruyere Waffles....................................29
10. Nutty Cocoa Cereal..31
11. Breakfast Tacos...33
12. Cheesy Bacon and Chive Omelet....................................35
13. Pizza Waffles..37
14. Anchovy, Spinach and Asparagus Omelet....................39
15. Autumn Zero-Belly Pumpkin Bread..............................41
16. Frozen Zero-Bellyccino..43
17. Sweet & Creamy Eggs..45
18. Zero-Belly Oatmeal...47
19. Batter Coated Cheddar Cheese.......................................49
20. Cheesy Boiled Eggs...51
21. Mahón Kale Sausage Omelet Pie....................................53
22. Monterey Bacon-Scallions Omelet.................................56
23. Smoked Turkey Bacon and Avocado Muffins..............58
24. Chorizo Breakfast Peppers...61
25. Creamy Chocó & Avocado Mousse................................64
26. Sour Cream Cheese Pancakes...66
27. Vesuvius Scrambled Eggs with Provolone...................68
28. Adorable Pumpkin Flaxseed Muffins............................70
29. Baked Ham and Kale Scrambled Eggs..........................72

30. Bell Pepper and Ham Omelet...75
31. Chia Flour Pancakes...77
32. Chocó Mocha Chia Porridge..79
33. Coffee Flaxseed Dream Breakfast.......................................81
34. Crimini Mushroom with Boiled Eggs Breakfast............83
35. Egg Whites and Spinach Omelet..85
SNACKS AND APPETIZERS...87
36. Pancetta & Eggs...88
37. Zero-Belly Margherita Pizza...90
38. Easy, Peasy, Cheese Pizza..92
39. Zero-Belly Trio Queso Quesadilla.....................................94
40. Bacon and Cheese Melt...96
41. BLT Roll..98
42. Portobello Pizza...100
43. Basil and Bell Pepper Pizza...102
POULTRY..105
44. Chicken Pie..106
45. Classic Chicken Parmigiana...109
46. Turkey Leg Roast...111
47. Slow-Cooked Greek Chicken...113
48. Roasted Bacon-Wrapped Chicken...................................115
49. Crispy Curried Chicken...117
50. The Perfect Baked Chicken Wings..................................119
51. Chicken in Kung Pao Sauce...121
52. Chicken BBQ Pizza...124
53. Slow Cooked Chicken Masala...126
54. Baked Buttered Chicken..128
55. Chicken Parmesan..130
SEAFOOD...133
56. Sweet and Sour Snapper..134
57. Creamy Haddock..136
58. Pan Fried Hake..138
59. Pesto and Almond Salmon..140
60. Lime Avocado Salmon...142
61. Glazed Sesame Ginger Salmon..144

62. Buttery Shrimp..146
63. Zero-Belly Friendly Sushi..149
64. Stuffed Avocado with Tuna..151
65. Herb Baked Salmon Fillets...153
66. Salmon with a Walnut Crust..156
67. Baked Glazed Salmon...158
68. Salmon Burgers...160
SOUPS AND STEWS...162
69. Rosemary Garlic Beef Stew..163
70. Bouillabaisse Fish Stew..166
71. Beef & Broccoli Stew...169
72. Mussel Stew..171
73. Creamy Chicken & Pumpkin Stew..................................174
74. Sweet Potato Stew..176
75. Beef Shin Stew..178
76. Tuna Fish Stew...181
77. Cauliflower and Cheese Chowder....................................183
78. Chicken Bacon Chowder..186
DESSERTS..189
79. Morning Zephyr Cake..190
80. Peanut Butter Balls..192
81. Pecan Flax Seed Blondies...194
82. Peppermint Chocolate Ice Cream....................................197
83. Puff-up Coconut Waffles..199
84. Raspberry Chocolate Cream...201
85. Raw Cacao Hazelnut Cookies..203
86. Sinless Pumpkin Cheesecake Muffins.............................205
87. Sour Hazelnuts Biscuits with Arrowroot Tea...............207
88. Tartar Zero-Belly Cookies...209
89. Wild Strawberries Ice Cream..211
90. Mini Lemon Cheesecakes...213
91. Fudgy Peanut Butter Squares...215
92. Lemon Squares & Coconut Cream.................................217
93. Rich Almond Butter Cake & Chocolate Sauce..............219
94. Peanut Butter Cake Covered in Chocolate Sauce.......221

SMOOTHIES..223
95. Green Coconut Smoothie...224
96. Green Devil Smoothie...226
97. Green Dream Zero-Belly Smoothie..................................228
98. Zero-Belly Celery and Nut Smoothie...............................230
99. Lime Peppermint Smoothie..232
100. Red Grapefruit Kale Smoothies......................................234
CONCLUSION...236

INTRODUCTION

Welcome to the Zero Belly Cookbook! In this collection of nourishing recipes, we invite you to embark on a journey towards a healthier you. The Zero Belly approach focuses on nourishing your body with wholesome ingredients that promote a balanced metabolism, help burn fat, and support overall well-being. This cookbook is your guide to creating delicious meals that will help you achieve your health and fitness goals.

At Zero Belly, we believe that food can be both nourishing and satisfying. We've curated a collection of recipes that prioritize ingredients that are high in nutrients and flavor, while being low in added sugars, unhealthy fats, and artificial ingredients. These recipes are designed to help you optimize your metabolism, support healthy digestion, and achieve a leaner, healthier body.

Within these pages, you will find a variety of mouthwatering recipes that encompass a range of flavors, textures, and cuisines. From hearty breakfasts and vibrant salads to flavorful main courses and guilt-free desserts, we've created a diverse collection of meals that will keep you satisfied and energized throughout your day. Each recipe is carefully crafted to provide you with a balance of macronutrients, vitamins, and minerals, while still being delicious and easy to prepare.

But this cookbook is more than just a compilation of healthy recipes. We'll guide you through the principles of the Zero Belly approach, share tips on ingredient selection, provide strategies for meal planning, and offer insights into the science behind nourishing your body for optimal health. Our goal is to empower you to make informed choices about the foods you eat, and to create a sustainable and enjoyable approach to healthy eating.

So, whether you're looking to shed a few pounds, boost your energy levels, or simply adopt a healthier lifestyle, let the Zero Belly Cookbook be your companion on this journey. Get ready to nourish your body with delicious meals that will transform the way you look, feel, and live.

BREAKFASTS

1. Zero-Belly Pancakes and Syrup

Total Time: 30 MIN | Serve: 5

INGREDIENTS:
FOR SYRUP:
- 2 tbsp maple syrup, sugar-free
- ½ cup Sukrin fiber syrup

FOR PANCAKES:
- 4 eggs, large
- 2 tbsp erythritol
- ½ tsp baking soda
- 3/4 cup nut butter of your choice
- 1/3 cup coconut milk
- 2 tbsp ghee
- 1 tsp cinnamon

INSTRUCTIONS:
- Add maple syrup and sukrin fiber syrup into a jar or small bowl and use a spoon to stir until combined. Cover jar and put aside until needed.
- Put eggs, erythritol, baking soda, coconut milk, nut butter and cinnamon powder in a food processor and pulse until blended.
- Heat ghee in a non-stick skillet and use about a ¼ cup per pancake. Cook until pancake sets then flip and finish cooking; place on a plate.
- Repeat with remaining batter and plate.
- Top with syrup and serve.

NUTRITION: Calories 401 | Total Fats 32.5g | Net Carbs: 3.6g | Protein 12.8g | Fiber 5.3g)

2.Bacon Avocado Breakfast Muffins

Total Time: 41 MIN| Serve: 16)

INGREDIENTS:
- ½ cup almond flour
- 1 ½ tbsp psyllium husk powder
- 4.5 oz Colby jack cheese
- 1 tsp baking powder
- 1 tsp garlic, diced
- 1 tsp chives, dried
- 3 stalks spring onions
- 1 tsp cilantro, dried
- ¼ tsp red chili flakes
- Salt and pepper
- 1 ½ tbsp lemon juice
- 5 eggs
- ¼ cup flaxseed meal
- 1 ½ cup coconut milk, from box
- 5 slices bacon, cut into strips
- 2 avocados, cubed
- 2 tbsp butter, organic

INSTRUCTIONS:
- Add flour, spices, lemon juice, eggs, flaxseed meal and coconut milk to a bowl. Mix together until thoroughly combined.
- Heat a skillet and cook bacon strips until crispy then add the butter and avocado.
- Add the bacon and avocado mixture to batter and mix together.
- Set oven to 350 F and grease cupcake molds.

- Add batter to molds and bake for 26 minutes. Take from oven and cool before removing from mold.
- Serve. Store leftovers in the fridge.

NUTRITION: Calories 163 | Total Fats 14.1g | Net Carbs: 1.5g | Protein 6.1g | Fiber 3.3g)

3. Orange Cinnamon Scones

Total Time: 30 MIN| Serve: 8)

INGREDIENTS:
- 1 tbsp golden flax seed
- 1 ½ tsp cinnamon
- ½ tsp salt
- 7 tbsp + 1 tbsp coconut flour
- ½ tsp baking powder
- Zest from one orange
- ¼ cup butter, unsalted, cubed
- ¼ cup erythritol
- ¼ tsp stevia
- 2 eggs
- 2 tbsp maple syrup
- ½ tsp xanthan gum
- 1/3 cup heavy cream
- 1 tsp vanilla

FOR ICING:
- 20 drops stevia
- 1 tbsp orange juice
- ¼ cup coconut butter

INSTRUCTIONS:
- Set oven to 400 F.
- Place all dry ingredients in a bowl except xanthan and 1 tbsp coconut flour. Add butter to dry mix and stir to combine.
- Combine sweetener and eggs until thoroughly mixed and light in color. Put in maple syrup, remaining flour, xanthan gum, heavy cream and vanilla; mix until combined and thick.

- Add wet mixture to dry, reserving 2 tbsp of liquids, mix together and add cinnamon and use hands to form mixture into dough. Shape into a ball and press into a cake like a shape. Slice into 8 pieces.
- Place onto a lined baking sheet and use reserved liquid to brush the top of scones.
- Bake for 15 minutes, remove from oven and cool.
- Prepare icing and drizzle over scones before serving.

NUTRITION: Calories 232 | Total Fats 20g | Net Carbs: 3.3g | Protein 3.3g | Fiber: 4.3 g)

4.Red Pepper, Mozzarella and Bacon Frittata

Total Time: 35 MIN| Serve: 6

INGREDIENTS:
- 1 tbsp olive oil
- 7 slices bacon
- 1 red bell pepper, chopped
- ¼ cup heavy cream
- ¼ cup parmesan cheese, grated
- 9 eggs
- Salt and pepper
- 2 tbsp parsley, chopped
- 4 cups Bella mushrooms, large
- ½ cup basil, chopped
- 4 oz mozzarella cheese, cubed
- 2 oz goat cheese, chopped

INSTRUCTIONS:
- Set oven to 350 F.
- Heat olive oil in a skillet then add bacon and cook for 5 minutes until browned.
- Add red pepper and cook for 2 minutes until soft. While pepper cooks, add cream, parmesan cheese, eggs, parsley, salt, and pepper to a bowl and whisk to combine.
- Add mushrooms to pot, stir and cook for 5 minutes until soaked in fat. Add basil, cook for 1 minute then add mozzarella.
- Add in egg mixture and use a spoon to move ingredients around so that the egg gets on the bottom of the pan.
- Top with goat cheese and place in oven for 8 minutes then broil for 6 minutes.

- Use a knife to pry frittata edges from pan and place on a plate and slice.

NUTRITION: Calories 408 | Total Fats 31.2g | Net Carbs: 2.4g | Protein 19.2g |Fiber: 0.8g)

5. Cheese and Sausage Pies

Total Time: 40 MIN| Serve: 2

INGREDIENTS:
- 1 ½ pieces chicken sausage
- ½ tsp rosemary
- ¼ tsp baking soda
- ¼ cup coconut flour
- ¼ tsp cayenne pepper
- 1/8 tsp salt
- 5 egg yolks
- 2 tsp lemon juice
- ¼ cup coconut oil
- 2 tbsp coconut milk
- ¾ cheddar cheese, grated

INSTRUCTIONS:
- Set oven to 350 F.
- Chop sausage, heat skillet and cook sausage. While sausages cook combine all dry ingredients in a bowl. In another bowl combine egg yolks, lemon juice, oil and coconut milk. Add liquids to dry mixture and add ½ cup of cheese; fold to combine and put into 2 ramekins.
- Add cooked sausages to the batter and use a spoon to push into the mixture.
- Bake for 25 minutes until golden on top. Top with leftover cheese and broil for 4 minutes.
- Serve warm.

NUTRITION: Calories 711 | Total Fats 65.3g | Net Carbs: 5.8g | Protein 34.3g |Fiber: 11.5g)

6.Breakfast Quiche

Total Time: 30 MIN| Serve: 2

INGREDIENTS:
- 3 tbsp coconut oil
- 5 eggs
- 8 slices bacon, cooked and chopped
- ½ cup cream
- 2 cups baby spinach, roughly chopped
- 1 cup red pepper, chopped
- 1 cup yellow onion, chopped
- 2 cloves garlic, minced
- 1 cup mushrooms, chopped
- 1 cup cheddar cheese, grated
- Salt

INSTRUCTIONS:
- Preheat oven to 375 F.
- In a large bowl, mix all vegetables including the mushrooms together.
- In another small bowl, whisk the 5 eggs with the cream
- Carefully scoop the veggie mixture into a muffin pan coated with cooking spray, top with egg and cheese filling up to ¾ of the muffin tins. Sprinkle with chopped bacon on top.
- Place in the oven to bake for 15 minutes or until the top of the quiche are firm.
- Let it cool for a few minutes before serving.

NUTRITION: Calories 210 | Total Fats 13g | Net Carbs: 5g | Protein 6g)

7. Chicharrones con Huevos (Pork Rind and Eggs)

Total Time: 30 MIN| Serve: 3

INGREDIENTS:
- 4 slices bacon
- 1.5 oz pork rinds
- 1 avocado, cubed
- ¼ cup onion, chopped
- 1 tomato, chopped
- 2 jalapeno pepper, seeds removed and chopped
- 5 eggs
- ¼ cup cilantro
- Salt and pepper

INSTRUCTIONS:
- Heat skillet and cook bacon until slightly crisp. Remove from pot and put aside on paper towels.
- Add pork rinds to the pot along with onion, tomatoes, pepper and cook for 3 minutes until onions are soft and clear.
- Add cilantro, stir together gently and add eggs. Scramble eggs and then add avocado and fold.
- Serve.

NUTRITION: Calories 508 | Total Fats 43g | Net Carbs: 12g | Protein 5g |Fiber: 5.3g)

8. Raspberry & Cacao Breakfast Bowl

Total Time: 40 MIN | Serve: 1

INGREDIENTS:
- 1 cup almond milk
- 1 tbsp cacao powder
- 3 tbsp chia seeds
- ¼ cup raspberry
- 1 tsp agave or xylitol

INSTRUCTIONS:
- In a small bowl, combine the almond milk and cocoa powder. Stir well.
- Add the chia seeds to the bowl and let it rest for 5 minutes.
- Using a fork, fluff the chia and cacao mixture and then place in the fridge to chill for at least 30 minutes.
- Serve with raspberries and a drizzle of agave on top

NUTRITION: Calories 230 | Total Fats 20g | Net Carbs: 4g | Protein 15g)

9. Anaheim pepper Gruyere Waffles

Total Time: 16 MIN| Serve: 2

INGREDIENTS:
- 1 small Anaheim pepper
- 3 eggs
- 1/4 cup cream cheese
- 1/4 cup Gruyere cheese
- 1 tbsp coconut flour
- 1 tsp Metamucil powder
- 1 tsp baking powder
- Salt and pepper to taste

INSTRUCTIONS:
- In a blender, mix together all ingredients except for the cheese and Anaheim pepper. Once the ingredients are mixed well, add cheese and pepper. Blend well until all ingredients are mix well.
- Heat your waffle iron; pour on the waffle mix and cook 5-6 minutes. Serve hot.

NUTRITION: Calories 223.55 | Total Fats 17g | Net Carbs: 5.50g | Protein 11g)

10. Nutty Cocoa Cereal

Total Time: 12 MIN| Serve: 2

INGREDIENTS:
- 3 tsp organic butter
- ¾ cup toasted walnuts, roughly chopped
- ¾ cup toasted macadamia nuts, roughly chopped
- ½ cup coconut shreds, unsweetened
- ½ tbsp stevia (optional)
- 2 cups almond milk
- 1/8 tsp salt

INSTRUCTIONS:
- Melt the butter in a pot over the medium heat. Add the toasted nuts to the pot and stir for 2 minutes.
- Add the shredded coconut into the pot and continue stirring to make sure to not burn the ingredients.
- Drizzle with stevia (if using) and then pour the milk into the pot. Add salt. Stir again and turn the heat off.
- Allow resting for 10 minutes to allow the ingredients to soak in the milk before serving.

NUTRITION: Calories 515 | Total Fats 50.3g | Net Carbs: 14.4g | Protein 6.5g |Fiber: 7.3g)

11. Breakfast Tacos

Total Time: 25 MIN| Serve: 3

INGREDIENTS:
- 3 strips bacon
- 1 cup mozzarella cheese, shredded
- 2 tbsp butter
- 6 eggs
- Salt and pepper
- ½ avocado, cubed
- 1 oz cheddar cheese, shredded

INSTRUCTIONS:
- Cook bacon until crisp, put aside until needed.
- Heat a non-stick pan and place 1/3 cup mozzarella into the pan and cook for 3 minutes until browned around the edges. Place a wooden spoon in a bowl or pot and use tongs to lift cheese 'taco from the pot. Repeat with leftover cheese.
- Melt butter in a skillet and scramble eggs; use pepper and salt to season.
- Spoon eggs into hardened shells and top with avocado and bacon.
- Top with cheddar and serve.

NUTRITION: Calories 443 | Total Fats 36.2g | Net Carbs: 3g | Protein 25.7g |Fiber: 1.7g)

12.Cheesy Bacon and Chive Omelet

Total Time: 30 MIN | Serve: 1

INGREDIENTS:
- 2 eggs, large
- Salt and pepper
- 1 tsp bacon fat
- 1 oz cheddar cheese
- 2 slices bacon, cooked
- 2 stalks chives

INSTRUCTIONS:
- Beat eggs together and add pepper and salt to taste. Chop chives and shred cheese.
- Heat skillet and cook bacon fat until hot.
- Add eggs to pot and top with chives. Cook until edges start to set then add bacon and cook for 30-60 seconds.
- Add cheese and a few additional chives. Use a spatula to fold in half. Press to seal and flip over.
- Serve immediately.

NUTRITION: Calories 463 | Total Fats 39g | Net Carbs: 1g | Protein 24g | Fiber 0g)

13.Pizza Waffles

Total Time: 30 MIN| Serve: 2

INGREDIENTS:
- 1 tbsp psyllium husk
- 1 tsp baking powder
- Salt
- 3 oz cheddar cheese
- 4 eggs, large
- 3 tbsp almond flour
- 1 tbsp butter, organic
- 1 tsp Italian seasoning
- 4 tbsp parmesan cheese
- ½ cup tomato sauce

INSTRUCTIONS:
- Add all ingredients to a bowl except cheese and tomato sauce. Use mixer or immersion blender to combine until mixture is thick.
- Heat waffle iron and use mixture to make two waffles.
- Place waffles onto a lined baking sheet and top with tomato sauce and cheese (divide evenly). Broil for 3 minutes or until cheese melted.
- Serve.

NUTRITION: Calories 525.5 | Total Fats 41.5g | Net Carbs: 5g | Protein 29g | Fiber 5.5g)

14. Anchovy, Spinach and Asparagus Omelet

Total Time: 23 MIN| Serve: 2

INGREDIENTS:
- 2 oz anchovy in olive oil
- 2 organic eggs
- 3/4 cup of spinach
- 4 marinated asparagus
- Celtic Sea salt
- Freshly ground black pepper
-

INSTRUCTIONS:
- Preheat the oven to 375 F.
- In the bottom of the baking pan place the anchovy.
- In a bowl, beat the eggs and pour on top of the fish. Add the spinach and the chopped asparagus on top.
- Season with salt and pepper to taste.
- Bake in preheated oven for about 10 minutes.
- Serve hot.

NUTRITION: Calories 83 | Total Fats 4.91g | Net Carbs: 2.28g | Protein 7.5g)

15. Autumn Zero-Belly Pumpkin Bread

Total Time: 1 HR 30 MIN| Serve: 2

INGREDIENTS:
- 3 egg whites
- 1/2 cup coconut milk
- 1 1/2 cup almond flour
- 1/2 cup pumpkin puree
- 2 tsp baking powder
- 1 1/2 tsp Pumpkin pie spice
- 1/2 tsp Kosher Salt
- Coconut oil for greasing

INSTRUCTIONS:
- Preheat your oven to 350F. Grease a standard bread loaf pan with melted coconut oil.
- Sift all dry ingredients into a large bowl.
- In another bowl, add pumpkin puree and coconut milk and mix well. In a separate bowl, beat the egg whites. Fold in egg whites and gently fold into the dough.
- Spread the dough into the prepared bread pan.
- Bake the bread for 75 minutes. Once ready, remove bread from the oven and let cool.
- Slice and serve.

NUTRITION: Calories 197 | Total Fats 16g | Net Carbs: 8.18g | Protein 7.2g)

16. Frozen Zero-Bellyccino

Total Time: 10 MIN| Serve: 1

INGREDIENTS:
- 1 cup cold coffee
- 1/3 cup heavy cream
- 1/4 tsp xanthan gum
- 1 tsp pure vanilla extract
- 1 tbsp xylitol
- 6 ice cubes
-

INSTRUCTIONS:
- Place all of the ingredients in your blender.
- Blend until all ingredients are well combined and become smooth.
- Serve and enjoy.

NUTRITION: Calories 287 | Total Fats 29g | Net Carbs: 2.76g | Protein 1.91g)

17. Sweet & Creamy Eggs

Total Time: 17 MIN| Serve: 1

INGREDIENTS:
- 2 organic eggs
- 1/3 cup heavy cream, preferably organic
- ½ tbsp stevia
- 2 tbsp organic butter
- 1/8 tsp cinnamon, ground

INSTRUCTIONS:
- In a small bowl, whisk the eggs, whipping cream, and sweetener.
- Melt the organic butter in a pan over medium heat and then pour in the egg mixture.
- Stir and cook until the eggs start to thicken and then transfer into a bowl.
- Sprinkle with cinnamon on top before serving.

NUTRITION: Calories 561 | Total Fats 53.6g | Net Carbs: 6.4g | Protein 15g)

18. Zero-Belly Oatmeal

Total Time: 20 MIN | **Serve: 5**

INGREDIENTS:
- 1/3 cup almonds, flaked
- 1/3 cup unsweetened coconut flakes
- ¼ cup chia seeds
- 2 tbsp erythritol
- ¼ cup coconut, shredded, unsweetened
- 1 cup almond milk
- 1 tsp vanilla, sugar-free
- 10 drops stevia extract
- ½ cup heavy whipping cream, whipped

INSTRUCTIONS:
- Place almonds and coconut flakes in a pot and toast for 3 minutes until fragrant.
- Place toasted ingredients into a bowl along with chia seeds, erythritol, and shredded coconut; mix together to combine.
- Top with milk and stir. You can use hot or cold milk based on your preference.
- Add vanilla and stevia, stir and set aside for 5-10 minutes.
- Serve topped with whipped cream.

NUTRITION: Calories 277 | Total Fats 25.6g | Net Carbs: 16.4g | Protein 5.5g | Fiber: 7.5g)

19. Batter Coated Cheddar Cheese

Total Time: 23 MIN| Serve: 1

INGREDIENTS:
- 1 large egg
- 2 slices Cheddar cheese
- 1 tsp ground walnuts
- 1 tsp ground flaxseed
- 2 tsp almond flour
- 1 tsp hemp seeds
- 1 tbsp olive oil
- Salt and pepper to taste

INSTRUCTIONS:
- In a small bowl, whisk an egg together with the salt and pepper.
- Heat a tbsp of olive oil in a frying pan, on medium heat.
- In a separate bowl, mix the ground flaxseed with the ground walnuts, hemp seeds, and the almond flour.
- Coat the cheddar slices with the egg mix, then roll in the dry mix and fry cheese for about 3 minutes on each side. Serve hot.

NUTRITION: Calories 509 | Total Fats 16g | Net Carbs: 2g | Protein 21g)

20. Cheesy Boiled Eggs

Total Time: 27 MIN| Serve: 2

INGREDIENTS:
- 3 eggs
- 2 tbsp almond butter, no-stir
- 2 tbsp cream cheese, softened
- 1 tsp whipping cream
- Salt and pepper to taste

INSTRUCTIONS:
- In a small saucepan hard boil the eggs.
- When ready, wash the eggs with cold water, peel and chop them. Place eggs in a bowl; add in the butter, cream cheese and whipping cream.
- Mix well and add salt and pepper to taste. Serve.

NUTRITION: Calories 212 | Total Fats 19g | Net Carbs: 0.75g | Protein 7g)

21. Mahón Kale Sausage Omelet Pie

Total Time: 40 MIN| Serve: 8)

INGREDIENTS:
- 3 chicken sausages
- 2 1/2 cups mushrooms, chopped
- 3 cups fresh spinach
- 10 eggs
- 1/2 tsp black pepper and celery seed
- 2 tsp hot sauce
- 1 tbsp garlic powder
- Salt and pepper to taste
- 1 1/2 cups Mahón cheese (or Cheddar)

INSTRUCTIONS:
- Preheat oven to 400 F.
- Chop up the mushroom and chicken sausage thin and place them in a cast iron skillet. Cook on a medium-high heat for 2-3 minutes.
- While the sausages are cooking, chopped spinach, then add spinach and mushrooms to the skillet.
- In a meanwhile, in a bowl mix eggs with black pepper and celery seed, spices, and hot sauce. Scramble all mixture well.
- Mix your spinach, mushrooms, and sausages so that the spinach can wilt completely. Season with salt and pepper to taste.
- Finally, add the cheese to the top.
- Pour eggs over the mixture and combine well.
- Stir the mixture for a few seconds, and then place your skillet in the oven. Bake for 10-12 minutes, and then broil the top for 4 minutes.

- Let cool for a while, cut into 8 slices and serve hot.

NUTRITION: Calories 266 | Total Fats 17g | Net Carbs: 7g | Protein 19g)

22. Monterey Bacon-Scallions Omelet

Total Time: 30 MIN| Serve: 2

INGREDIENTS:
- 2 eggs
- 2 slices cooked bacon
- 1/4 cup scallions, chopped
- 1/4 cup Monterey Jack cheese
- Salt and pepper to taste
- 1 tsp lard

INSTRUCTIONS:
- In a frying pan heat lard in on medium-low heat. Add the eggs, scallions and salt and pepper to taste.
- Cook for 1-2 minutes; add the bacon and sauté 30 - 45 seconds longer. Turn the heat off on the stove.
- On top of the bacon place a cheese. Then, take two edges of the omelet and fold them onto the cheese. Hold the edges there for a moment as the cheese has to partially melt. Make the same with the other egg and let cook in a warm pan for a while.
- Serve hot.

NUTRITION: Calories 321 | Total Fats 28g | Net Carbs: 1.62g | Protein 14g)

23. Smoked Turkey Bacon and Avocado Muffins

Total Time: 45 MIN| Serve: 16)

INGREDIENTS:
- 6 slices smoked turkey bacon
- 2 tbsp butter
- 3 spring onions
- 1/2 cup cheddar cheese
- 1 tsp baking powder
- 1 1/2 cups coconut milk
- 5 eggs
- 1 1/2 tbsp Metamucil powder
- 1/2 cup almond flour
- 1/4 cup flaxseed
- 1 tsp minced garlic
- 2 tsp dried parsley
- 1/4 tsp red chili powder
- 1 1/2 tbsp lemon juice
- Salt and pepper to taste
- 2 medium avocados

INSTRUCTIONS:
- Preheat oven to 350 F.
- In a frying pan over medium-low heat, cook the bacon with the butter until crisp. Add the spring onions, cheese, and baking powder.
- In a bowl, mix together coconut milk, eggs, Metamucil powder, almond flour, flax, spices and lemon juice. Switch off the heat and let cool. Then, crumble the bacon and add all of the fat to the egg mixture.
- Clean and chop avocado and fold into the mixture.

- Measure out batter into a cupcake tray that's been sprayed or greased with nonstick spray and bake for 25-26 minutes.
- Once ready, let cool and serve hot or cold.

NUTRITION: Calories 184 | Total Fats 16g | Net Carbs: 5.51g | Protein 5.89g)

24. Chorizo Breakfast Peppers

Total Time: 25 MIN| Serve: 2

INGREDIENTS:
- ½ tbsp ghee
- 1 onion, chopped
- 2 cloves of garlic
- 6 organic eggs
- ¼ cup almond milk, unsweetened
- 1 cup cheddar cheese, shredded
- Salt and pepper to taste
- 3 large bell peppers, cut in half, core and seeds removed
- ½ lb. spicy chorizo sausage, crumbled

INSTRUCTIONS:
- Set oven to 350 F.
- Heat the ghee in a non-stick pan over medium heat and cook the chorizo crumbles. Set aside
- Using the same pan, add the onions and garlic and sauté for a few minutes. Turn off the heat and set aside.
- In a bowl, stir together the eggs, milk, cheddar, and season with salt and pepper.
- Add the chorizo into the bowl with the eggs and stir well.
- Place the bell pepper halves in an oven-safe dish filled with a ¼ inch of water.
- Scoop the chorizo and egg mixture into the bell peppers and place the dish into the oven to bake for 35 minutes.
- Serve warm.

NUTRITION: Calories 631 | Total Fats 46g | Net Carbs: 13g | Protein 44g | Fiber: 3.5 g)

25. Creamy Chocó & Avocado Mousse

Total Time: 50 MIN| Serve: 2

INGREDIENTS:
- 2 ripe avocados
- 1/3 cup cocoa powder
- ½ tsp chia seeds
- 1 tsp vanilla extract
- 10 drops Stevie
- 3 tbsp coconut oil

INSTRUCTIONS:
- Place all the ingredients in a blender and blend until smooth.
- Pour the mixture into a bowl and place in the fridge to chill for 40 minutes or more.
- Serve chilled.

NUTRITION: Calories 462 | Total Fats 46g | Net Carbs: 15g | Protein 6g | Fiber 1.2 g)

26. Sour Cream Cheese Pancakes

Total Time: 30 MIN| Serve: 2

INGREDIENTS:
- 2 eggs
- 1/4 cup cream cheese
- 1 tbsp coconut flour
- 1 tsp ground ginger
- 1/2 cup liquid Stevie
- Coconut oil
- Sugar-free maple syrup

INSTRUCTIONS:
- In a deep bowl, beat together all of the ingredients until smooth.
- Heat up a frying skillet with oil on medium-high. Ladle the batter and pour in hot oil.
- Cook on one side and then flip. Top with a sugar-free maple syrup and serve.

NUTRITION: Calories 170 | Total Fats 13g | Net Carbs: 4g | Protein 6.90g)

27. Vesuvius Scrambled Eggs with Provolone

Total Time: 15 MIN| Serve: 2

INGREDIENTS:
- 2 large eggs
- 3/4 cup Provolone cheese
- 1.76 oz. air-dried salami
- 1 tsp fresh rosemary (chopped)
- 1 tbsp olive oil
- Salt and pepper to taste
-

INSTRUCTIONS:
- In a small pan with olive oil fry the chopped salami.
- In the meantime, in a small bowl whisk the eggs, then add the salt, pepper and fresh rosemary.
- Add in the provolone cheese and mix well with a fork.
- Pour the egg mixture into the pan with salami and cook for about 5 minutes. Serve hot.

NUTRITION: Calories 396 | Total Fats 32.4g | Net Carbs: 2.8g | Protein 26.1g | Fiber: 0.3 g)

28. Adorable Pumpkin Flaxseed Muffins

Total Time: 25 MIN| Serve: 2

INGREDIENTS:
- 1 egg
- 1 1/4 cups flax seeds (ground)
- 1 cup pumpkin puree
- 1 tbsp pumpkin pie spice
- 2 tbsp coconut oil
- 1/2 cup sweetener of your choice
- 1 tsp baking powder
- 2 tsp cinnamon
- 1/2 tsp apple cider vinegar
- 1/2 tsp vanilla extract
- Salt to taste

INSTRUCTIONS:
- Preheat your oven to 360 F.
- First, grind the flaxseeds for several seconds.
- Put together all the dry ingredients and stir.
- Then, add your pumpkin puree and mix to combine.
- Add the vanilla extract and the pumpkin spice.
- Add in coconut oil, egg and apple vinegar. Add sweetener of your choice and stir again.
- Add a heaping tbsp of batter to each lined muffin or cupcake and top with some pumpkin seeds.
- Bake for about 18 - 20 minutes. Serve hot.

NUTRITION: Calories 43| Total Fats 5.34g | Net Carbs: 3g | Protein 1g | Fiber: 1 g)

29. Baked Ham and Kale Scrambled Eggs

Total Time: 40 MIN| Serve: 2

INGREDIENTS:
- 5 ounces ham diced
- 2 medium eggs
- 1 green onion, finely chopped
- 1/2 cups kale leaves, chopped
- 1 garlic clove, crushed
- 1 green chili, finely chopped
- 4 ready-roasted peppers
- Pinch cayenne pepper
- 1 tbsp olive oil
- 1/2 can water

INSTRUCTIONS:
- Heat oven to 360 F.
- Heat the oil in a small ovenproof frying pan. Add green onion and cook for 4-5 minutes until softened.
- Stir in the garlic and chili, and cook for a couple minutes more.
- Add the 1/2 cup water. Season well and stir in the ready-roasted peppers and ham. Bring to a simmer and cook for 10 minutes.
- Add the kale, stirring through to wilt.
- In a small bowl, beat the eggs with a pinch of cayenne and pour in frying pan together with other ingredients.
- Transfer the frying pan to the oven and bake for 10 minutes.
- Serve hot.

NUTRITION: Calories 251| Total Fats 15.74g | Net Carbs: 3.8g | Protein 22g | Fiber: 0.8g)

30. Bell Pepper and Ham Omelet

Total Time: 30 MIN| Serve: 2

INGREDIENTS:
- 4 large eggs
- 1 cup green pepper, chopped
- 1/4 lb ham, cooked and diced
- 1 green onion, diced
- 1 tsp coconut oil
- Salt and freshly ground pepper to taste

INSTRUCTIONS:
- Wash and chop vegetables. Set aside.
- Into a small bowl beat the eggs. Set aside.
- Heat a non-stick skillet over medium heat and add coconut oil. Pour half of the beaten eggs into the skillet.
- When the egg has partially set, add half of the vegetables and ham to one-half of the omelet and continue to cook until the egg is almost fully set.
- Fold the empty half over top of the ham and veggies using a spatula.
- Cook for 2 minutes more and then serve.
- Serve hot.

NUTRITION: Calories 225.76 | Total Fats 12g | Net Carbs: 6.8g | Protein 21.88g | Fiber: 1.4g)

31. Chia Flour Pancakes

Total Time: 25 MIN | Serve: 6

INGREDIENTS:
- 1 cup chia flour
- 2 tsp sweetener of your choice
- 1 egg, beaten
- 1 tbsp coconut butter or oil
- 1/2 cup coconut milk (canned)

INSTRUCTIONS:
- In a medium bowl, combine the flour and sweetener. Add the egg, milk and coconut butter. Mix well until make a smooth batter.
- Grease a non-stick skillet and heat over medium-high heat. Drop a heaping tbsp of batter onto the hot surface.
- When bubbles form on the surface of the scones, use a spatula to turn them and then cook about 2 minutes per side.
- Serve hot.

NUTRITION: Calories 59 | Total Fats 3.5g | Net Carbs: 4.65g | Protein 2.46g | Fiber: 1.78g)

32. Chocó Mocha Chia Porridge

Total Time: 35 MIN| Serve: 6

INGREDIENTS:
- 3 tbsp chia seeds
- 1 cup almond milk, unsweetened
- 2 tsp cocoa powder
- 1/4 cup raspberries, fresh or frozen
- 2 tbsp almond, ground
- Sweetener of your choice
-

INSTRUCTIONS:
- Mix and stir the almond milk and the cocoa powder together.
- Add the Chia Seeds in the mixture.
- Mix well with a fork.
- Place the mixture in a fridge for 30 minutes.
- Serve with raspberries and ground almonds on the top (optional)

NUTRITION: Calories 150.15 | Total Fats 9.62g | Net Carbs: 15.2g | Protein 5.47g | Fiber: 11.28g)

33. Coffee Flaxseed Dream Breakfast

Total Time: 10 MIN| Serve: 1

INGREDIENTS:
- 3 tbsp flaxseed, ground
- 2 1/2 tbsp coconut flakes, unsweetened
- 1/2 cup strong black coffee, unsweetened
- Sweetener of your choice to taste
- 1/2 cup water (optional)
-

INSTRUCTIONS:
- In a bowl, combine the flaxseed and the coconut flakes.
- Add the melted coconut oil, and then pour the hot coffee over it and mix.
- If it is too thick, add a little water.
- At the end, add the sweetener of your choice to taste.

NUTRITION: Calories 246.43 | Total Fats 22.1g | Net Carbs: 1.52g | Protein 1.48g | Fiber: 0.9g)

34. Crimini Mushroom with Boiled Eggs Breakfast

Total Time: 25 MIN| Serve: 6

INGREDIENTS:
- 14 crimini mushrooms, finely chopped
- 8 large eggs, hard-boiled, chopped
- 6 slices bacon or pancetta
- 1 spring onion, diced
- Salt and ground black pepper to taste

INSTRUCTIONS:
- In a frying pan cook bacon. Reserve a bacon fat in the pan. Chop up bacon pieces and set aside.
- In a deep saucepan, hard-boil the eggs. When ready, wash, clean, shell and chop into bite-size pieces.
- In a frying pan cook the spring onion with remaining bacon fat over medium-high heat.
- Add the Crimini mushrooms and sauté another 5-6 minutes.
- Blend the eggs, bacon and cook together. Adjust salt and ground black pepper to taste.
- Serve.

NUTRITION: Calories 176.15 | Total Fats 13.38g | Net Carbs: 2.43g | Protein 11.32g | Fiber: 1.5g)

35. Egg Whites and Spinach Omelet

Total Time: 25 MIN| Serve: 2

INGREDIENTS:
- 5 egg whites
- 2 tbsp almond milk
- 1 zucchini, shredded
- 1 cup spinach leaves, fresh
- 2 tbsp spring onion, chopped
- 2 cloves garlic
- Olive oil
- Basil leaves, fresh, chopped
- Salt and ground black pepper to taste

INSTRUCTIONS:
- Wash and chop the vegetables
- In a bowl, beat the egg whites and the almond milk.
- In a greased frying pan with olive oil, cook the vegetables (spinach, zucchini, and spring onion) just for one to two minutes.
- Put the vegetables on the side, grease the pan again with olive oil and pour the eggs. Cook until the eggs are firm. Add the vegetables on one side and cook for two minutes more. Adjust salt and pepper to taste.
- Decorate with basil leaves and serve.

NUTRITION: Calories 70.8 | Total Fats 1.56g | Net Carbs: 5.78g | Protein 11.08g | Fiber: 1.58g)

SNACKS AND APPETIZERS

36. Pancetta & Eggs

Total Time: 25 MIN| Serve: 4

INGREDIENTS:
- 4 large slices Pancetta
- 2 eggs, free-range
- 1 cup ghee, softened
- 2 Tbsp mayonnaise
- Salt and freshly ground black pepper to taste
- Coconut oil for frying

INSTRUCTIONS:
- In a greased non-stick frying pan, bake Pancetta from both sides 1-2 minutes. Remove from the fire and set aside.
- In a meanwhile boil the eggs. To get the eggs hard-boiled, you need around 10 minutes. When done, wash the eggs with cold water well and peel off the shells.
- In a deep bowl place ghee and add the quartered eggs. Mash with a fork well. Season it with salt and pepper to taste; add mayonnaise and mix. If you want you can pour in the Pancetta grease. Combine and mix well. Place the bowl in the fridge for one hour at least.
- Remove the egg mixture from the fridge and make 4 equal balls.
- Crumble the Pancetta into small pieces. Roll each ball in the Pancetta crumbles and place on a big platter.
- Remove the Egg and Pancetta bombs in a fridge for 30 minutes more. Serve cold.

NUTRITION: Calories 238 | Total Fats 22g | Net Carbs: 0.5g | Protein 7.5g)

37. Zero-Belly Margherita Pizza

Total Time: 20 MIN| Serve: 2

INGREDIENTS:
FOR THE CRUST:
- 2 organic eggs
- 2 tbsp parmesan cheese, grated
- 1 tbsp psyllium husk powder
- 1 tsp Italian seasoning
- ½ tsp salt
- 2 tsp ghee

FOR THE TOPPINGS:
- 5 basil leaves, roughly chopped
- 2 oz. mozzarella cheese, sliced
- 3 tbsp all-natural tomato sauce

INSTRUCTIONS:
- Place all the ingredients for the crust in a food processor and pulse until well combined.
- Pour the mixture into a hot non-stick pan and tilt to spread the batter.
- Cook until the edges are brown. Flip to the other side and cook for another 45 seconds. Remove from the heat.
- Spread the tomato sauce on top of the crust, add the mozzarella and basil leaves on top and place in the broiler to melt the cheese for 2 minutes.
- Serve.

NUTRITION: Calories 459 | Total Fats 35g | Net Carbs: 3.5g | Protein 27g)

38. Easy, Peasy, Cheese Pizza

Total Time: 35 MIN| Serve: 3

INGREDIENTS:
- 2 whole eggs
- 1 cup cheddar cheese, grated
- 1 tbsp psyllium husk
- 3 tbsp pesto sauce

INSTRUCTIONS:
- Preheat oven to 350 F.
- Mix eggs and cheese along with the psyllium husk in a bowl and combine well.
- Place the mixture on baking paper and spread quite thinly. Place in the oven to cook for 15-20 minutes. Remember to keep an eye on it, as it gets brown and crispy quickly relative to the thickness, don't make it too thin.
- Once cooked, remove from the oven and place whatever you wish over the base, like the pesto sauce or tomato sauce.
- Top with your favorite pizza toppings such as bacon slices, pepperoni chicken, fresh tomato, and fresh basil.

NUTRITION: Calories 335 | Total Fats 27g | Net Carbs: 3.2g | Protein 18g)

39. Zero-Belly Trio Queso Quesadilla

Total Time: 20 MIN| Serve: 1

INGREDIENTS:
- ¼ cup pepper jack cheese, shredded
- ¼ cup sharp cheddar cheese, shredded
- 1 cup mozzarella cheese, cheese
- 2 tbsp coconut flour
- 1 organic egg
- ½ tsp garlic powder
- 1 tbsp almond milk, unsweetened

INSTRUCTIONS:
- Set the oven at 350 F.
- Microwave the mozzarella in the microwave until it starts to melt.
- Allow the mozzarella to cool before adding the coconut flour, egg, garlic powder, and milk.
- Stir well until you achieve a dough-like consistency.
- Place the dough in between two parchment papers and roll flat.
- Remove the top parchment paper, transfer the dough to a baking sheet, and place in the oven to bake for 10 minutes.
- Take out from the oven and allow to cool for a few minutes before topping with the cheeses on one-half of the prepared tortilla.
- Fold in half and place back in the oven to cook for 5 minutes or until the cheese has melted.

NUTRITION: Calories 977 | Total Fats 73g | Net Carbs: 12g | Protein 63g)

40. Bacon and Cheese Melt

Total Time: 15 MIN| Serve: 2

INGREDIENTS:
- 8 pcs string mozzarella cheese sticks
- 8 strips of bacon
- Olive oil for frying

INSTRUCTIONS:
- Preheat your deep fryer to 350 F.
- Wrap a cheese stick with one strip of bacon and secure with a toothpick. Repeat until you've used all the bacon and cheese.
- Deep fry the cheese sticks in the fryer for 3 minutes.
- Remove and place on top of a paper towel.
- Serve with a leafy green salad on the side.

NUTRITION: Calories 590 | Total Fats 50g | Net Carbs: 0g | Protein 34g)

41. BLT Roll

Total Time: 10 MIN| Serve: 1

INGREDIENTS:
- 4 leaves, romaine lettuce
- 4 bacon strips, cooked and crumbled
- 4 slices deli turkey
- 1 cup cherry tomatoes cut in half
- 2 tbsp mayonnaise

INSTRUCTIONS:
- Lay the turkey slice on top of the lettuce leaves.
- Spread mayonnaise on the turkey slice and then top with the cherry tomatoes and bacon on top.
- Roll the lettuce and then secure with a toothpick.
- Serve immediately.

NUTRITION: Calories 382 | Total Fats 38.5g | Net Carbs: 11.5g | Protein 4.1g | Fiber 6.3g)

42. Portobello Pizza

Total Time: 25 MIN| Serve: 4

INGREDIENTS:
- 1 medium tomato, sliced
- ¼ cup basil, chopped
- 20 pepperoni slices
- 4 Portobello mushroom caps
- 4 oz mozzarella cheese
- 6 tbsp olive oil
- Black pepper
- Salt

INSTRUCTIONS:
- Remove insides of mushrooms and take out meat so that the shell is left.
- Coat mushrooms with half of oil and season with pepper and salt; broil for 5 minutes then turn over and coat with leftover oil. Bake for an additional 5 minutes.
- Add tomato to the inside of shell and top with basil, pepperoni, and cheese. Broil for 4 minutes until cheese melts.
- Serve warm.

NUTRITION: Calories 321 | Total Fats 31g | Net Carbs: 2.8g | Protein 8.5g | Fiber 1.3g)

43. Basil and Bell Pepper Pizza

Total Time: 30 MIN| Serve: 2

INGREDIENTS:
FOR BASE:
- ½ cup almond flour
- 2 tsp cream cheese
- 1 egg
- ½ tsp salt
- 6 oz mozzarella cheese
- 2 tbsp psyllium husk
- 2 tbsp parmesan cheese
- 1 tsp Italian seasoning
- ½ tsp black pepper

FOR TOPPINGS:
- 1 medium tomato, sliced
- 2/3 bell pepper, sliced
- 4 oz cheddar cheese, shredded
- ¼ cup tomato sauce
- 3 tbsp basil, chopped

INSTRUCTIONS:
- Preheat oven to 400 F. Place mozzarella into a microwave safe dish and melt for 1 minute, stirring occasionally.
- Add cream cheese to melted mozzarella and combine.
- Mix dry ingredients for base together in a bowl, add egg and combine. Add cheese mixture and use hands to combine into a dough.
- Form dough into a circle, bake for 10 minutes and remove from oven. Top with tomato sauce, tomato, basil, bell pepper and cheddar cheese.

- Return to oven and bake for 10 additional minutes.
- Serve warm.

NUTRITION: Calories 410 | Total Fats 31.3g | Net Carbs: 5.3g | Protein 24.8g | Fiber 5.8g)

POULTRY

44. Chicken Pie

Total Time: 30 MIN| Serve: 5

INGREDIENTS:
- ½ lb. boneless chicken thighs cut into small pieces
- 3.5 oz bacon, chopped
- 1 carrot, chopped
- ¼ cup parsley, chopped
- 1 cup heavy cream
- 2 onion leeks, chopped
- 1 cup white wine
- 1 tbsp olive oil
- Salt and pepper to taste

FOR THE CRUST
- 1 cup almond meal
- 2 tbsp water
- 1 tbsp stevia
- 1½ tbsp butter
- ½ tsp salt

INSTRUCTIONS:
- Prepare the crust first by combining all its ingredients. Set aside.
- Heat the olive oil in a pan over the medium-high fire. Throw in the chopped leeks and stir. Transfer to a plate.
- Throw in the chicken meat and bacon and cook until brown and add the leeks.
- Add the carrots and pour the white wine and then reduce the heat to medium.
- Add the parsley and pour the heavy cream in stir well. Transfer into a baking dish.

- Cover with the prepared crust and place in the oven to cook until the crust turns golden brown and crispy.
- Allow resting for 20 minutes before serving.

NUTRITION: Calories 396| Total Fats 33g | Net Carbs: 6.5g | Protein 12.1g | Fiber: 2.5 g)

45. Classic Chicken Parmigiana

Total Time: 50 MIN| Serve: 2

INGREDIENTS:
- 2 pcs boneless chicken thighs
- 8 strips of bacon, chopped
- ½ cup parmesan cheese, grated
- ½ cup mozzarella cheese, shredded
- 1 organic egg
- 1 canned diced tomato

INSTRUCTIONS:
- Set the oven at 450 F.
- Tenderize the chicken and set aside.
- Place the parmesan cheese on a plate.
- Crack the egg into a bowl and whisk. And dip the chicken in it.
- Transfer to the plate with cheese and coat the chicken with the parmesan.
- Grease the baking sheet with butter, place the chicken thighs and bake in the oven for 30-40 minutes.
- While waiting for the chicken to bake, cook the bacon.
- Pour the tomatoes with the bacon and stir. Reduce the heat to low and allow simmering and reducing.
- Remove the chicken from the oven when done and ladle over the tomato sauce.
- Sprinkle with the mozzarella on top and place back in the oven to melt the cheese.
- Serve hot.

NUTRITION: Calories 826 | Total Fats 50.3g | Net Carbs: 6.2g | Protein 83.2g | Fiber: 1.2g)

46. Turkey Leg Roast

Total Time: 1 HR 20 MIN| Serve: 4

INGREDIENTS:
- 2 pcs turkey legs
- 2 tbsp ghee

FOR THE RUB:
- $\frac{1}{4}$ tsp cayenne
- $\frac{1}{2}$ tsp thyme, dried
- $\frac{1}{2}$ tsp ancho chili powder
- $\frac{1}{2}$ tsp garlic powder
- $\frac{1}{2}$ tsp onion powder
- 1 tsp liquid smoke
- 1 tsp Worcestershire
- Salt and pepper to taste

INSTRUCTIONS:
- Set the oven at 350 F.
- Combine all the ingredients for the rub in a bowl. Whisk well.
- Dry the turkey legs with a clean towel and generously rub it with the spice mixture.
- Heat the ghee over a medium-high fire in a cast iron skillet and then sear the turkey legs for 2 minutes on each side.
- Place the turkey in the oven to bake for one hour.

NUTRITION: Calories 382 | Total Fats 22.5g | Net Carbs: 0.8g | Protein 44g | Fiber: 0.0g)

47. Slow-Cooked Greek Chicken

Total Time: 7 HR 10 MIN| Serve: 4

INGREDIENTS:
- 4 pcs boneless chicken thighs
- 3 cloves of garlic, minced
- 3 tbsp lemon juice
- 1 ½ cups hot water
- 2 cubes chicken bouillon
- 3 tbsp Greek Rub

INSTRUCTIONS:
- Coat the slow cooker with cooking spray
- Season the chicken with the Greek rub followed by the minced garlic.
- Transfer the chicken to the slow cooker and sprinkle with lemon juice on top.
- Crumble the chicken cubes and put in the slow cooker. Pour the water and stir.
- Cover and cook on low for 6-7 hours.

NUTRITION: Calories 140 | Total Fats 5.7g | Net Carbs: 2.2g | Protein 18.6g)

48. Roasted Bacon-Wrapped Chicken

Total Time: 1 HR 25 MIN| Serve: 6

INGREDIENTS:
- 1 whole dressed chicken
- 10 strips of bacon
- 3 sprigs fresh thyme
- 2 pcs lime
- Salt and pepper to taste

INSTRUCTIONS:
- Set the oven at 500 F.
- Thoroughly rinse the chicken and stuff it with the lime and thyme sprigs.
- Season the chicken with salt and pepper and then wrap the chicken with the bacon.
- Season again with salt and pepper and then place on a roasting tray on top of a baking sheet (make sure to catch the juices) and place in the oven to roast for 15 minutes.
- Lower the temperature to 350 F and then roast for another 45 minutes.
- Remove the chicken from the oven, cover with foil and set aside for 15 minutes.
- Take the juices from the tray and place in a saucepan. Bring to a boil over high heat and use an immersion blending to mix all the "good stuff" from the juice.
- Serve the chicken with the sauce on the side.

NUTRITION: Calories 375 | Total Fats 29.8g | Net Carbs: 2.4g | Protein 24.5g | Fiber: 0.9g)

49. Crispy Curried Chicken

Total Time: 60 MIN | Serve: 4

INGREDIENTS:
- 4 pcs chicken thighs
- ¼ cup olive oil
- 1 tsp curry powder
- ¼ tsp ginger
- ½ tsp cumin, ground
- ½ tsp smoked paprika
- ½ tsp garlic powder
- ¼ tsp cayenne
- ¼ tsp allspice
- ¼ tbsp chili powder
- Pinch of coriander, ground
- Pinch of cinnamon
- Pinch of cardamom
- ½ tsp salt

INSTRUCTIONS:
- Set the oven at 425 F.
- Combine all the spices together.
- Line a baking sheet with foil and lay the chicken on it.
- Drizzle the chicken with olive oil, and rub.
- Sprinkle the spice mixture on top and then rub again, make sure to coat the chicken with the spices.
- Place in the oven to bake for 50 minutes.
- Allow to rest for 5 minutes before serving.

NUTRITION: Calories 277 | Total Fats 19.9g | Net Carbs: 0.6g | Protein 42.3g)

50. The Perfect Baked Chicken Wings

Total Time: 40 MIN | Serve: 2

INGREDIENTS:
- 2.5 lbs chicken wings
- ½ tsp baking soda
- 1 tsp baking powder
- Salt to taste
- 4 tbsp butter, melted

INSTRUCTIONS:
- Add all the ingredients (except butter) in a Ziploc bag and shake, making sure that the wings are coated with the mixture.
- Place in the fridge overnight.
- When you're ready to cook, set the oven at 450 F.
- Place the wings on a baking sheet and cook in the oven for 20 minutes.
- Flip the wings and bake for another 15 minutes.
- Melt the butter and drizzle over the wings.

NUTRITION: Calories 500 | Total Fats 0.0g | Net Carbs: 38.8g | Protein 44g | Fiber: 34g)

51. Chicken in Kung Pao Sauce

Total Time: 25 MIN| Serve: 2

INGREDIENTS:
- 2 boneless chicken thighs cut into smaller pieces
- ½ green pepper, chopped
- 2 pcs spring onions, sliced thin
- ¼ cup peanuts, chopped
- 1 tsp ginger, grated
- ½ tbsp red chili flakes
- Salt and pepper to taste

FOR THE SAUCE:
- 2 tsp rice wine vinegar
- 1 tbsp Zero-Belly Ketchup
- 2 tbsp chili garlic paste
- 1 tbsp low-sodium soy sauce
- 2 tsp sesame oil
- 2 tsp liquid stevia
- ½ tsp maple syrup

INSTRUCTIONS:
- Season the chicken with salt, pepper, and grated ginger.
- Place a cast iron skillet over the medium-high fire and add the chicken when the pan is hot. Cook for 10 minutes.
- Whisk all the ingredients for the sauce in a bowl while waiting for the chicken to cook.
- Add the green pepper, spring onions, and peanuts to the pan with the chicken, and cook for another 4-5 minutes
- Add the sauce to the pan stir and allow to boil.

NUTRITION: Calories 362 | Total Fats 27.4g | Net Carbs: 3.2g | Protein 22.3g)

52. Chicken BBQ Pizza

Total Time: 20 MIN| Serve: 4

INGREDIENTS:
- 1 cup roasted chicken, shredded
- 4 tbsp BBQ sauce
- ½ cup cheddar cheese
- 1 tbsp mayonnaise
- 4 tbsp all-natural tomato sauce

FOR THE PIZZA CRUST
- 6 tbsp parmesan cheese, grated
- 6 organic eggs
- 3 tbsp psyllium husk powder
- 2 tsp Italian seasoning
- Salt and pepper to taste

INSTRUCTIONS:
- Set oven to 425 F.
- Place all the ingredients for the crust in a food processor and pulse until you achieve a thick dough.
- Shape the pizza dough and place in the oven to cook for 10 minutes.
- Top the cooked crust with the tomato sauce followed by the chicken, cheese, and a drizzle of the BBQ sauce and mayonnaise on top.

NUTRITION: Calories 357 | Total Fats 24.5g | Net Carbs: 2.9g | Protein 24.5g)

53. Slow Cooked Chicken Masala

Total Time: 3 HR 10 MIN| Serve: 2

INGREDIENTS:
- 1 ½ lb. boneless chicken thighs, sliced into small pieces
- 2 cloves of garlic
- 1 tsp ginger, grated
- 1 tsp onion powder
- 3 tbsp masala
- 1 tsp paprika
- 2 tsp salt
- ½ cup coconut milk (divided into 2)
- 2 tbsp tomato paste
- ½ cup diced tomatoes
- 2 tbsp olive oil
- ½ cup heavy cream
- 1 tsp stevia
- Fresh cilantro for garnish

INSTRUCTIONS:
- Place the chicken first in the slow cooker. Add the grated ginger, garlic, and the rest of the spices. Stir.
- Add the tomato paste and diced tomatoes next and stir again.
- Pour the ½ of the coconut milk and mix and then cook on high for 3 hours.
- When done the cooking, add the remaining coconut milk, heavy cream, stevia, and mix again.
- Serve hot.

NUTRITION: Calories 493 | Total Fats 41.2g | Net Carbs: 5.8g | Protein 26g)

54. Baked Buttered Chicken

Total Time: 1 HR 10 MIN| Serve: 2

INGREDIENTS:
- 4 pcs chicken thighs
- ¼ cup softened organic butter
- 1 tsp rosemary, dried
- 1 tsp basil, dried
- ½ tsp salt
- ½ tsp pepper

INSTRUCTIONS:
- Set oven to 350 F.
- Whisk all the ingredients (except the chicken) in a bowl.
- Place the chicken thighs on a baking sheet lined with foil and generously brush it with the butter mixture.
- Place the chicken in the oven to bake for an hour.
- Serve warm.

NUTRITION: Calories 735 | Total Fats 33.7g | Net Carbs: 0.8g | Protein 101.8g)

55. Chicken Parmesan

Total Time: 25 MIN| Serve: 4

INGREDIENTS:
FOR CHICKEN:
- 3 Chicken breasts
- 1 cup Mozzarella cheese
- Salt
- Black pepper

FOR COATING:
- ¼ cup Flaxseed meal
- 1 tsp Oregano
- ½ tsp Black pepper
- ½ tsp Garlic powder
- 1 Egg
- 2.5 oz Pork rinds
- ½ cup Parmesan cheese
- ½ tsp Salt
- ¼ tsp Red pepper flakes
- 2 tsp Paprika
- 1 ½ tsp Chicken broth

FOR SAUCE:
- 1 cup tomato sauce, low carb
- 2 Garlic Cloves
- Salt
- ½ cup Olive oil
- ½ tsp Oregano
- Black pepper

INSTRUCTIONS:
- Add flax meal, spices, pork rinds and parmesan cheese in a processor and grind until combined.

- Pound chicken breast and whisk egg with broth in a container. Add all ingredients for the sauce to a pan stir and put over a low flame to cook.
- Dip chicken in egg and then coat with dry mixture.
- Heat oil in a pan and fry chicken then transfer to a casserole dish. Top with sauce and mozzarella and bake for 10 minutes.

NUTRITION: Calories 646 | Total Fats 46.8g | Net Carbs: 4g | Protein 49.3g|Fiber 2.8g)

SEAFOOD

56. Sweet and Sour Snapper

Total Time: 20 MIN| Serve: 2

INGREDIENTS:
- 4 fillets snapper
- ¼ cup fresh coriander, chopped
- 4 tbsp juice of lime
- 6 pcs lychees, sliced
- 2 tbsp olive oil
- Salt and pepper to taste

INSTRUCTIONS:
- Season the filets with salt and pepper.
- Heat the olive oil in a pan over medium heat and cook for 4 minutes on each side.
- Drizzle the lime juice on the fish; add the coriander, and the sliced lychees.
- Reduce the heat to low and allow to cook for another 5 minutes.
- Transfer to a serving plate and enjoy.

NUTRITION: Calories 244 | Total Fats 15.4g | Net Carbs: 0.1g | Protein 27.9g)

57. Creamy Haddock

Total Time: 20 MIN| Serve: 2

INGREDIENTS:
- 5.3 oz smoked haddock
- 1/2 boiling water
- 1 tbsp butter
- ¼ cup cream
- 2 cups spinach

INSTRUCTIONS:
- Heat a saucepan over medium fire.
- Mix the boiling water with cream and butter in a bowl.
- Place haddock and sauce in the pan and leave to boil until the water evaporates, leaving a creamy, butter sauce behind.
- Serve haddock, covered with the sauce on fresh or wilted spinach.

NUTRITION: Calories 281 | Total Fats 10g | Net Carbs: 15g | Protein 18g)

58. Pan Fried Hake

Total Time: 15 MIN| Serve: 1

INGREDIENTS:
- 1 tbsp olive oil
- Salt and pepper to taste
- 1 Hake fillet
- Fresh lemon wedges

INSTRUCTIONS:
- Heat the olive oil in a large frying pan over medium-high heat.
- Pat the fish dry with kitchen paper towel and then season with salt and pepper on both sides.
- Fry the fish for about 4-5 minutes on each side, depending on their thickness, or until they have a golden crust and the flesh flakes away easily with a fork.

NUTRITION: Calories 170 | Total Fats 8g | Net Carbs: 7g | Protein 18g)

59. Pesto and Almond Salmon

Total Time: 15 MIN| Serve: 2

INGREDIENTS:
- 1 Garlic clove
- ½ Lemons
- ½ Tsp Parsley
- 2 Tbsp Butter
- Handful Frisée
- 1 Tbsp Olive oil
- ¼ Cup Almonds
- ½ Tsp Himalayan salt
- 12 oz. Salmon filets
- ½ Shallots

INSTRUCTIONS:
- Add almonds, garlic and olive oil to a processor and pulse until mixture is pasty. Add parsley, salt and squeeze lemon juice into mixture and put aside until needed.
- Season salmon with pepper and salt.
- Heat oil in a skillet and place skin of salmon into pot and cook for 3 minutes per side.
- Add butter to skillet and heat until melted; coat fish with butter and remove from heat.
- Serve salmon with frisée and pesto.

NUTRITION: Calories 610 | Total Fats 47g | Net Carbs: 6g | Protein 38g |Fiber: 1g)

60. Lime Avocado Salmon

Total Time: 25 MIN | Serve: 2

INGREDIENTS:
- 1 Avocado
- 2 Tbsp Red onions (chopped)
- $\frac{1}{2}$ Cup Cauliflower
- 12 oz. Salmon filets (2)
- $\frac{1}{2}$ Limes

INSTRUCTIONS:
- Place cauliflower in a processor and pulse until texture is similar to rice.
- Grease skillet with cooking spray and add rice to skillet, cook for 8 minutes with the lid on.
- Add remaining ingredients except for fish to a food processor and blend until creamy and smooth.
- Heat your choice of oil in another skillet and place filets with skin down in the pot. Cook for 5 minutes and add pepper and salt to taste. Flip and cook for 5 minutes more.
- Serve salmon with cauliflower and top with avocado sauce.

NUTRITION: Calories 420 | Total Fats 27g | Net Carbs: 5g | Protein 37g | Fiber: 0.5g)

61. Glazed Sesame Ginger Salmon

Total Time: 40 MIN | Serve: 2

INGREDIENTS:
- 2 tbsp Soy sauce
- 1 tbsp Rice wine vinegar
- 2 tsp Garlic, grated
- 1 tbsp Ketchup
- 10 oz Salmon filet
- 2 tsp Sesame oil
- 1 tsp Ginger, diced
- 1 tbsp Fish sauce
- 2 tbsp White wine

INSTRUCTIONS:
- Combine soy sauce, vinegar, garlic, ginger, and fish sauce in a bowl and add salmon. Marinate for 15 minutes.
- Heat sesame oil in a skillet until smoking then add fish with skin down into the pan. Cook for 4 minutes then flip over and cook for an additional 4 minutes or until done.
- Add marinade to the pot and cook for 4 minutes, remove from pot and set aside.
- Add white and ketchup to the sauce and cook for 5 minutes until reduced.
- Serve fish with sauce.

NUTRITION: Calories 370 | Total Fats 23.5g | Net Carbs: 2.5g | Protein 33g)

62. Buttery Shrimp

Total Time: 25 MIN| Serve: 3

INGREDIENTS:
FOR BATTERED SHRIMP:
- 2 tbsp Almond Flour
- ¼ tsp Curry powder
- 1 Egg
- 3 tbsp Coconut oil
- 0.5 oz Parmigiano- Reggiano
- ½ tsp Baking powder
- 1 tbsp Water
- 12 medium Shrimp

FOR BUTTER SAUCE:
- ½ Onion, chopped
- 2 Thai chilies, chopped
- ½ cup Heavy cream
- Salt
- 2 tbsp Butter, unsalted
- 1 Garlic clove, diced
- 2 tbsp Curry leaves
- 0.3 oz mature cheddar
- Black pepper
- 1/8 tsp Sesame seeds

INSTRUCTIONS:
- Peel and devein shrimp; dry shrimp using a paper towel.
- Combine all dry ingredients for batter then add water and egg and mix thoroughly to combine.
- Heat coconut oil in a skillet, dip shrimps into the batter and fry until golden. Take from the pot and put aside to cool.

- Melt butter in another pot and sauté onion until browned. Add curry leaves, chilies, and garlic and cook for 3 minutes or until aromatic.
- Lower heat and add cream and cheddar, cook until sauce thickens. Add shrimp and toss to coat.
- Serve topped with sesame seeds.

NUTRITION: Calories 570 | Total Fats 56.2g | Net Carbs: 18.4g | Protein 4.3g | Fiber 1.4g)

63. Zero-Belly Friendly Sushi

Total Time: 25 MIN | Serve: 3

INGREDIENTS:
- 16 oz Cauliflower
- 2 tbsp Rice vinegar, unseasoned
- 5 sheets Nori
- ½ Avocado, sliced
- 6 oz cream cheese, softened
- 1 tbsp Soy sauce
- Cucumber
- 5 oz Smoked salmon

INSTRUCTIONS:
- Put cauliflower into a food processor and pulse until a rice-like consistency is achieved.
- Slice each end of cucumber off and slice each side off, throw away center and slice sides into strips. Place in fridge until needed.
- Heat a skillet and add cauliflower and soy sauce. Cook for 5 minutes or until fully cooked and slightly dried out.
- Transfer cauliflower to the bowl along with vinegar and cheese, combine and place in refrigerator until chilled. Slice avocados and put aside.
- Cover bamboo roller with plastic wraps them lay down a sheet of nori, top with cooked cauliflower, salmon, cucumber, and avocados. Roll and slice.
- Serve.

NUTRITION: Calories 353 | Total Fats 25.7g | Net Carbs: 5.7g | Protein 18.32g | Fiber: 8g)

64. Stuffed Avocado with Tuna

Total Time: 20 MIN| Serve: 4

INGREDIENTS:
- 2 ripe avocados, halved and pitted
- 1 can (15 oz.) solid white tuna packed in water, drained
- 2 Tbsp mayonnaise
- 3 green onions, thinly sliced
- 1 Tbsp cayenne paprika
- 1 red bell pepper, chopped
- 1 Tbsp balsamic vinegar
- 1 pinch garlic salt and black pepper to taste
-

INSTRUCTIONS:
- In a bowl, toss together tuna, mayonnaise, cayenne pepper, green onions, red pepper, and balsamic vinegar.
- Season with pepper and salt, and then pack the avocado halves with the tuna mixture.
- Ready! Serve and enjoy!

NUTRITION: Calories 233.3| Total Fats 17.77g | Net Carbs: 9.69g | Protein 7.41g | Fiber: 6.98g)

65. Herb Baked Salmon Fillets

Total Time: 35 MIN| Serve: 6

INGREDIENTS:
- 2 lbs. salmon fillets
- 1/2 cup chopped fresh mushrooms
- 1/2 cup chopped green onions
- 4 oz. butter
- 4 Tbsp coconut oil
- 1/2 cup tamari soy sauce
- 1 tsp minced garlic
- 1/4 tsp thyme
- 1/2 tsp rosemary
- 1/4 tsp tarragon
- 1/2 tsp ground ginger
- 1/2 tsp basil
- 1 tsp oregano leaves

INSTRUCTIONS:
- Preheat oven to 350 degrees F. Line a large baking pan with foil.
- Cut salmon filet into pieces. Put the salmon into the Ziploc bag with the tamari sauce, sesame oil, and spices sauce mixture. Refrigerate the salmon and marinade it for 4 hours.
- Put the salmon in a baking pan and bake fillets for 10-15 minutes.
- Melt the butter. Add the chopped fresh mushrooms and green onion to it, and mix. Remove the salmon from the oven, and pour the butter mixture over the salmon fillets, making sure each fillet gets covered.
- Bake for about 10 minutes more. Serve immediately.

NUTRITION: Calories 449 | Total Fats 34g | Net Carbs: 2.7g | Protein 33g | Fiber 0.7g)

66. Salmon with a Walnut Crust

Total Time: 20 MIN| Serve: 2

INGREDIENTS:
- ½ cup Walnuts
- ½ tbsp Dijon mustard
- 6 oz Salmon filets
- Salt
- 2 tbsp Maple syrup, sugar-free
- ¼ tsp Dill
- 1 tbsp Olive oil

INSTRUCTIONS:
- Set oven to 350 F.
- Put mustard, syrup, and walnuts into a processor and pulse until mixture is pasty.
- Heat oil in a pot and place the skin side down in the pan and sear for 3 minutes.
- Top it with walnut blend and place into a lined baking dish.
- Bake for 8 minutes.
- Serve.

NUTRITION: Calories 373 | Total Fats 43g | Net Carbs: 3g | Protein 20g | Fiber 1g)

67. Baked Glazed Salmon

Total Time: 30 MIN| Serve: 2

INGREDIENTS:
- 2 pcs salmon fillets
- For the glaze:
- 1 tbsp sweet mustard
- 1 tbsp Dijon mustard
- 1 tbsp lemon juice
- $\frac{1}{2}$ tsp chili flakes
- 1 tsp sage
- Salt to taste
- 1 tbsp olive oil

INSTRUCTIONS:
- Set the oven at 350 F.
- In a bowl whisk all the ingredients for the glaze.
- Place the salmon fillets on a baking sheet lined with parchment paper and brush the salmon fillets with the glaze.
- Place in the oven to bake for 20 minutes. Serve warm.

NUTRITION: Calories 379 | Total Fats 24.9g | Net Carbs: 4.3g | Protein 35.5g)

68. Salmon Burgers

Total Time: 20 MIN| Serve: 4

INGREDIENTS:
- 1 14.oz can cook salmon flakes in water
- 2 organic eggs
- 1 cup gluten-free breadcrumbs
- 1 small onion, chopped
- 1 tbsp fresh parsley, chopped
- 3 tbsp mayonnaise
- 2 tsp lemon juice
- Salt to taste
- 1 tbsp olive oil
- 1 tbsp ghee

INSTRUCTIONS:
- Crack the eggs into a bowl and use a hand mixer to whisk them until fluffy.
- Add the bread crumbs in the bowl with the egg and combine well.
- Add the onions, parsley, and mayonnaise and mix again.
- Add the salmon flakes, and drizzle the lemon juice and olive oil. Season with salt and stir again.
- Divide the mixture into 4 parts and then create patties using your hands.
- Heat the ghee in a cast iron skillet over the medium-high fire and fry the patties until golden brown.
- Serve with a salad on the side.

NUTRITION: Calories 281 | Total Fats 25.2g | Net Carbs: 9.1g | Protein 6.2g | Fiber 0.8g)

SOUPS AND STEWS

69. Rosemary Garlic Beef Stew

Total Time: 4 HR 20 MIN| Serve: 8)

INGREDIENTS:
- 4 medium carrots, sliced
- 4 sticks celery, sliced
- 1 medium onion, diced
- 2 tbsp olive oil
- 4 garlic cloves, minced
- 1.5 lbs beef stewing meat (shin or chuck)
- Salt and pepper
- ¼ cup almond flour
- 2 cups beef stock
- 2 tbsp Dijon mustard
- 1 tbsp Worcestershire sauce
- 1 tbsp soy sauce
- 1 tbsp xylitol
- ½ tbsp dried rosemary
- ½ tsp thyme

INSTRUCTIONS:
- Add onion, carrots, and celery into a slow cooker.
- Add stewing meat in a large bowl and season with pepper and salt.
- Add the almond flour and toss the meat until well coated.
- Fry the garlic in the hot oil for about one minute.
- Add the seasoned meat and all the flour from the bottom of the bowl to the pan.
- Cook the meat without stirring for a few minutes to allow it to brown on one side.

- Flip and repeat until all the sides of the beef are browned.
- Add the browned beef to the slow cooker and stir to combine with the vegetables.
- Add the beef stock, Dijon mustard, Worcestershire sauce, soy sauce, xylitol, thyme, and rosemary to the skillet.
- Stir to combine all ingredients and dissolve the browned bits from the bottom of the skillet.
- Once everything is dissolved then pour the sauce over the ingredients in the slow cooker.
- Cover slow cooker with lid and cook on high for four hours.
- After cooking, remove the lid and stir stew well and using dork shred the beef into pieces.

NUTRITION: Calories 275 | Total Fats 10g | Net Carbs: 24g | Protein 22g)

70. Bouillabaisse Fish Stew

Total Time: 6 HR 55 MIN| Serve: 6

INGREDIENTS:
- 1 cup dry white wine
- juice and zest of 1 orange
- 2 tbsp olive oil
- 1 large onion, diced
- 2 cloves garlic, minced
- 1 tsp dried basil
- 1/2 tsp dried thyme
- 1/2 tsp salt
- 1/4 tsp ground black pepper
- 4 cups fish stock; chicken stock can also be used
- 1 can diced tomatoes, drained
- 1 bay leaf
- 0.9 lb boneless, skinless white fish fillet (ex. cod)
- 0.9 lb prawns peeled and deveined
- 0.9 lb mussels in their shells
- Juice of 1/2 lemon
- 1/4 cup fresh Italian (flat-leaf) parsley

INSTRUCTIONS:
- Heat the oil in a large pan.
- Add the onion and fry all the vegetables until almost tender.
- Add the garlic, basil, thyme, salt, and pepper.
- Pour the wine and bring to a boil. Add the fish stock, orange zest, tomatoes, and bay leaf and stir to combine.
- Pour everything into a slow cooker, cover the cooker, and cook on low for 4 to 6 hours.

- About 30 minutes before serving, turn the cooker to high. Toss the fish and prawns with the lemon juice.
- Stir into the broth in the cooker, cover, and cook until the fish cooks through about 20 minutes.
- Add mussel's right at the end and allow to steam for 20 minutes with the lid on.

NUTRITION: Calories 310 | Total Fats 30g | Net Carbs: 4g | Protein 3g)

71. Beef & Broccoli Stew

Total Time: 2 HR 20 MIN| Serve: 8)

INGREDIENTS:
- 1 cup beef stock
- 1/4 cup soy sauce
- 1/4 cup oyster sauce
- 1/4 cup Xylitol
- 1 tbsp sesame oil
- 3 cloves garlic, minced
- 2.2 lbs boneless beef chuck roast and thinly sliced
- 2 tbsp almond flour or psyllium husk
- 2 heads broccoli, cut into florets

INSTRUCTIONS:
- In a medium bowl, whisk together beef stock, soy sauce, oyster sauce, sugar, sesame oil, and garlic.
- Place beef into a slow cooker. Add sauce mixture and gently toss to combine. Cover and cook on low heat for 90 minutes.
- In a small bowl, whisk together 1/4 cup water and almond flour.
- Stir in almond flour mixture and broccoli into the slow cooker.
- Cover and cook on high heat for an additional 30 minutes.

NUTRITION: Calories 370 | Total Fats 18g | Net Carbs: 4g | Protein 47g)

72. Mussel Stew

Total Time: 5 HR 45 MIN| Serve: 8)

INGREDIENTS:
- 2.2 lbs fresh or frozen, cleaned mussels
- 3 tbsp olive oil
- 4 cloves garlic, minced
- 1 Large onion, finely diced
- 1 punnet mushrooms, diced
- 2 cans diced tomatoes
- 2 tbsp oregano
- $\frac{1}{2}$ tbsp basil
- $\frac{1}{2}$ tsp black pepper
- 1 tsp paprika
- Dash red chili flakes
- 3/4 cup water

INSTRUCTIONS:
- Fry onions, garlic, shallots and mushrooms, scrape entire contents of the pan into your crockpot.
- Add all remaining ingredients to your slow cooker except your mussels. Cook on low for 4-5 hours, or on high for 2-3 hours. You're cooking until your mushrooms are fork tender and until the flavors meld together.
- Once your mushrooms are cooked and your sauce is done, crank the crockpot up to high. Add cleaned mussels to the pot and secure lid tightly. Cook for 30 more minutes.
- Ladle your mussels into bowls with plenty of broth. If any mussels didn't open up during cooking, toss those as well

NUTRITION: Calories 228 | Total Fats 9g | Net Carbs: 32g | Protein 4g)

73. Creamy Chicken & Pumpkin Stew

Total Time: 5 HR| Serve: 6

INGREDIENTS:
- 1.3 lb chicken boneless chicken breast
- 1 1/4 cups chicken stock
- 1 can evaporate milk (Full Cream)
- 1/3 cup of sour cream or crème Fraiche
- 1 tbsp minced garlic
- ½ cup grated mature cheddar cheese
- Fresh or frozen finely chopped pumpkin
- Salt and pepper to taste

INSTRUCTIONS:
- In a crockpot combine all ingredients.
- Cover and turn crock pot on low. Cook for 4.5 hours on low or until both chicken and pumpkin are cooked and soft.
- Stir sauce in crock pot prior to serving.

NUTRITION: Calories 321 | Total Fats 12g | Net Carbs: 17g | Protein 35g)

74. Sweet Potato Stew

Total Time: 6 HR 20 MIN | Serve: 6

INGREDIENTS:
- 2 cups cubed sweet potatoes
- 4 boneless chicken breasts
- 4 boneless chicken thighs
- 2 cups chicken stock
- 1 ½ cups chopped green sweet peppers
- 1 ¼ cup diced fresh tomatoes
- ¾ cup can tomatoes, onion and chili mix
- 1 tbsp Cajun or curry seasoning
- 2 cloves garlic, minced
- ¼ cup creamy nut
- Fresh coriander
- Chopped roasted nuts

INSTRUCTIONS:
- In a slow cooker sweet potatoes, chicken, broth, peppers, diced tomatoes, tomatoes and green chilies mix, Cajun seasoning, and garlic.
- Cover and cook on low-heat setting for 10 to 12 hours or on high-heat setting for 5 to 6 hours.
- Remove 1 cup hot liquid from cooker. Whisk the liquid with nut butter in a bowl. Add mixture in cooker.
- Serve topped with cilantro and, if desired, peanuts.

NUTRITION: Calories 399 | Total Fats 21g | Net Carbs: 13.5g | Protein 37g)

75. Beef Shin Stew

Total Time: 3 HR 25 MIN| Serve: 8)

INGREDIENTS:
- 2 lb. quality shin of beef, cubed
- 4 tbsp olive oil
- 2 red onions, peeled and roughly chopped
- 3 pcs carrots, peeled and roughly chopped
- 3 sticks celery, trimmed and roughly chopped
- 4 cloves garlic, unpeeled
- a few sprigs of fresh rosemary
- 2 bay leaves
- 2 cups mushrooms
- 2 cups baby marrows
- Salt and pepper to taste
- 1 tbsp psyllium husk
- 2 cans tomatoes
- ⅔ Bottle red wine

INSTRUCTIONS:
- Preheat your oven to 360 F.
- In a heavy-bottomed oven-proof saucepan, heat olive oil and sauté the onions, carrots, celery, garlic, herbs, and mushrooms for 5 minutes until softened slightly.
- Meanwhile, roll the beef in psyllium husk.
- Then add meat into saucepan and stir until all ingredients are mixed.
- Add the tomatoes, wine and a pinch of salt and pepper and gently bring to the boil.
- Once boiling, turn off the heat and cover the saucepan with double thickness tinfoil and the lid.

- Place saucepan in the oven to cook and develop flavor for 3 hours or until the beef can be pulled apart with a spoon.
- Taste and add more salt if necessary.
- Serve and enjoy.

NUTRITION: Calories 315 | Total Fats 7g | Net Carbs: 7g | Protein 20g)

76. Tuna Fish Stew

Total Time: 25 MIN| Serve: 2

INGREDIENTS:
- 1 tin tuna in water, drained
- 1 tbsp butter
- ¼ small onion, chopped finely
- 1 clove garlic, minced
- 1tsp fresh ginger, grated
- ½ tin tomatoes, chopped finely
- 1 cup spinach, chopped finely
- 1 small carrot, grated
- 1 tsp curry powder 1 tsp turmeric
- ½ tsp cayenne pepper (optional)
- Salt & pepper to taste

INSTRUCTIONS:
- Fry onion, garlic, and ginger in butter.
- Add tomatoes once onions are soft.
- Pieces and enough water to make a stew for the spinach, carrot and tuna fish. Cook at low heat for about 15 minutes.
- Do not overcook spinach.
- Steam 2 cups of cauliflower, mash and add 1Tblsp of butter. Serve stew on top of the caulimash.

NUTRITION: Calories 253 | Total Fats 5g | Net Carbs: 7g | Protein 25g |Fiber: 2g)

77. Cauliflower and Cheese Chowder

Total Time: 30 MIN| Serve: 4

INGREDIENTS:
- 4 cups cauliflower florets, chopped
- 4 bacon strips
- 1 tbsp organic butter
- 2 cloves of garlic, minced
- 1 onion, chopped fine
- ¼ cup almond flour
- 4 cups low-sodium chicken broth
- ½ cup milk
- ¼ cup light cream
- 1 cup cheddar, shredded
- Salt and pepper to taste

INSTRUCTIONS:
- Cook the bacon in a large pot. Remove from the pot when cooked and set aside.
- Using the same pot set the heat on medium and throws in the onions. Cook for 3 minutes and then add the garlic and cauliflower florets and cook for another 5 minutes.
- Add the flour into the pot and continuously whisk for a minute.
- Pour the chicken broth, milk, and light cream and stir for 3 minutes.
- Allow to simmer for 15 minutes and then turn off the heat.
- Add the cheddar cheese into the pot, season with salt and pepper and stir again.
- Serve with the chopped bacon on top.

NUTRITION: Calories 268 | Total Fats 15.9g | Net Carbs: 11.9g | Protein 19.5g | Fiber: 3.1 g)

78. Chicken Bacon Chowder

Total Time: 8 HR s10 MIN| Serve: 5

INGREDIENTS:
- 4 cloves garlic – minced
- 1 leek – cleaned, trimmed, and sliced
- 2 ribs celery – diced
- 1 punnet button mushrooms – sliced
- 2 medium sweet onion – thinly sliced
- 4 tbsp butter
- 2 cups chicken stock
- 6 boneless, skinless chicken breasts, butterflied
- 8 oz. cream cheese
- 1 cup heavy cream
- 1 packet streaky bacon – cooked crisp, and crumbled
- 1 tsp salt
- 1 tsp pepper
- 1 tsp garlic powder
- 1 tsp thyme

INSTRUCTIONS:
- Select low setting on your slow cooker.
- Place 1 cup of chicken stock, onions, garlic, mushroom, leeks, celery, 2 tbsps of butter, and the salt and pepper into your slow cooker.
- Put the lid on, and cook ingredients on low for 1 hour.
- Brown chicken breasts in a skillet with 2 tbsp of butter.
- Add the remaining 1 cup of chicken stock.
- Scrape the bottom of the skillet to remove any chicken that may have stuck to the bottom.

- Remove from skillet and set aside, pouring the fat from the pan over the chicken.
- Add in the thyme, heavy cream, garlic powder and cream cheese into your slow cooker.
- Stir the contents of the slow cooker until the cream cheese has melted into the dish.
- Cut the chicken into cubes. Add the bacon and chicken cubes into the slow cooker. Stir ingredients and cook on low for 6-8 hours.

NUTRITION: Calories 355 | Total Fats 21g | Net Carbs: 6.4g | Protein 28g)

DESSERTS

79. Morning Zephyr Cake

Total Time: 40 MIN| Serve: 8)

INGREDIENTS:
- 3 Tbsp coconut oil
- 2 Tbsp grounded flax seeds
- 8 Tbsp almonds, grounded
- 1 cup Greek Yogurt
- 1 Tbsp cocoa powder for dusting
- 1 cup heavy whipping cream
- 1 tsp Baking Powder
- 1 tsp Baking Soda
- 1 tsp pure vanilla essence
- 1 pinch pink salt
- 1 cup Stevia or Erythritol sweetener

INSTRUCTIONS:
- Pre-heat the oven to 350 F degrees.
- In the blender first add the grounded almonds, grounded flax seeds, and the baking powder and soda. Blend for a minute.
- Add the salt, coconut oil and blend some more. Add the sweetener and blend for 2-3 minutes.
- Add the Greek yogurt and blend for a minute or so, until a fine consistency is reached.
- Take out the batter in a bowl and add the vanilla essence, and mix with a light hand.
- Grease the baking dish and drop the batter in it.
- Bake for 30 minutes. Let cool on a wire rack. Serve.

NUTRITION: Calories 199.84 | Total Fats 20.69g | Net Carbs: 3.22g | Protein 2.56g | Fiber 1.17g)

80. Peanut Butter Balls

Total Time: 22 MIN| Serve: 16)

INGREDIENTS:
- 2 eggs
- 2 1/2 cup of peanut butter
- 1/2 cup shredded coconut (unsweetened)
- 1/2 cup of Xylitol
- 1 Tbsp of pure vanilla extract

INSTRUCTIONS:
- Preheat oven to 320 F.
- Mix all ingredients together by your hands.
- After the ingredients are thoroughly mixed, roll into heaped tbsp sized balls and press into a baking tray lined with baking paper.
- Bake in preheated oven for 12 minutes.
- When ready, let cool on a wire rack.
- Serve and enjoy.

NUTRITION: Calories 254.83 | Total Fats 21.75g | Net Carbs: 8.31g | Protein 10.98g | Fiber 2.64g)

81. Pecan Flax Seed Blondies

Total Time: 40 MIN| Serve: 16)

INGREDIENTS:
- 3 eggs
- 2 1/4 cups pecans, roasted
- 3 Tbsp heavy cream
- 1 Tbsp salted caramel syrup
- 1/2 cup flax seeds, ground
- 1/4 cup butter, melted
- 1/4 cup erythritol, powdered
- 10 drops Liquid Stevia
- 1 tsp baking powder
- 1 pinch salt

INSTRUCTIONS:
- Preheat oven to 350F.
- In a baking pan roast pecans for 10 minutes.
- Grind 1/2 cup flax seeds in a spice grinder. Place flax seed powder in a bowl. Grind Erythritol in a spice grinder until powdered. Set in the same bowl as the flax seed meal.
- Place 2/3 of roasted pecans in food processor and process until a smooth nut butter is formed.
- Add eggs, liquid Stevia, salted caramel syrup, and a pinch of salt to the flax seed mixture. Mix well. Add pecan butter to the batter and mix again.
- Crush the remaining roasted pecans into chunks.
- Add crushed pecans and 1/4 cup melted butter into the batter.
- Mix batter well and then add heavy cream and baking powder. Mix everything together well.

- Place the batter into baking tray and bake for 20 minutes.
- Let cool for about 10 minutes.
- Cut into square and serve.

NUTRITION: Calories 180.45 | Total Fats 18.23g | Net Carbs: 3.54g | Protein 3.07g | Fiber 1.78g)

82. Peppermint Chocolate Ice Cream

Total Time: 35 MIN| Serve: 3

INGREDIENTS:
- 1/2 tsp Peppermint extract
- 1 cup heavy cream
- 1 cup cheese cream
- 1 tsp pure vanilla extract
- 1 tsp Liquid Stevia extract
- 100% Dark Chocolate for topping

INSTRUCTIONS:
- Place ice cream bowl in the freezer.
- In a metal bowl, add all ingredients except chocolate and whisk well.
- Put back in the freezer for 5 minutes.
- Set up ice cream maker and add liquid.
- Before serving, top the ice cream with chocolate shavings. Serve.

NUTRITION: Calories 286.66 | Total Fats 29.96g | Net Carbs: 2.7g | Protein 2.6g)

83. Puff-up Coconut Waffles

Total Time: 20 MIN| Serve: 8)

INGREDIENTS:
- 1 cup coconut flour
- 1/2 cup heavy (whipping) cream
- 5 eggs
- 1/4 tsp pink salt
- 1/4 tsp baking soda
- 1/4 cup coconut milk
- 2 tsp Yacon Syrup
- 2 Tbsp coconut oil (melted)

INSTRUCTIONS:
- In a large bowl add the eggs and beat with an electric hand mixer for 30 seconds.
- Add the heavy (whipping) cream and coconut oil into the eggs while you are still mixing. Add the coconut milk, coconut flour, pink salt and baking soda. Mix with the hand mixer for 45 seconds on low speed. Set aside.
- Heat up your waffle maker well and make the waffles according to your manufactures specifications.
- Serve hot.

NUTRITION: Calories 169.21 | Total Fats 12.6g | Net Carbs: 9.97g | Protein 4.39g | Fiber 0.45g)

84. Raspberry Chocolate Cream

Total Time: 15 MIN| Serve: 4

INGREDIENTS:
- 1/2 cup 100% dark chocolate, chopped
- 1/4 cup of heavy cream
- 1/2 cup cream cheese, softened
- 2 Tbsp sugar-free Raspberry Syrup
- 1/4 cup Erythritol

INSTRUCTIONS:
- In a double boiler melt chopped chocolate and the cream cheese. Add the Erythritol sweetener and continue to stir. Remove from heat, let cool and set aside.
- When the cream has cooled add in heavy cream and Raspberry syrup and stir well.
- Pour cream in a bowls or glasses and serve. Keep refrigerated.

NUTRITION: Calories 157.67 | Total Fats 13.51g | Net Carbs: 7.47g | Protein 1.95g | Fiber 1g)

85. Raw Cacao Hazelnut Cookies

Total Time: 6 HR| Serve: 24)

INGREDIENTS:
- 2 cups almond flour
- 1 cup chopped hazelnuts
- 1/2 cup cacao powder
- 1/2 cup ground flax
- 3 Tbsp coconut oil (melted)
- 1/3 cup water
- 1/3 cup Erythritol
- 1/4 tsp liquid Stevia

INSTRUCTIONS:
- In a bowl, mix flax and almond flour, cacao powder.
- Stir in oil, water, agave, and vanilla. When it is well combined, stir in chopped hazelnuts.
- Form into balls, press flat with palms and place on dehydrator screens.
- Dehydrate one hour at 145, then reduce to 116 and dehydrate for at least five hours.
- Serve and enjoy.

NUTRITION: Calories 181.12 | Total Fats 15.69g | Net Carbs: 8.75g | Protein 4.46g | Fiber: 3.45 g)

86. Sinless Pumpkin Cheesecake Muffins

Total Time: 15 MIN | Serve: 6

INGREDIENTS:
- 1/2 cup pureed pumpkin
- 1 tsp pumpkin pie spice
- 1/2 cup pecans, finely ground
- 1/2 cup cream cheese
- 1 Tbsp coconut oil
- 1/2 tsp pure vanilla extract
- 1/4 tsp pure Yacon Syrup or Erythritol

INSTRUCTIONS:
- Prepare a muffin tin with liners.
- Place a few ground pecans into every muffin tin and make a thin crust.
- In a bowl, blend sweetener, spices, vanilla, coconut and the pumpkin puree. Add in the cream cheese and beat until the mixture is well combined.
- Scoop about two tbsp of filling mixture on top of each crust, and smooth the edges.
- Pop in the freezer for about 45 minutes.
- Remove from the muffin tin and let sit for 10 minutes. Serve.

NUTRITION: Calories 157.34 | Total Fats 15.52g | Net Carbs: 3.94g | Protein 2.22g | Fiber: 1.51g)

87. Sour Hazelnuts Biscuits with Arrowroot Tea

Total Time: 50 MIN| Serve: 12

INGREDIENTS:
- 1 egg
- 1/2 cup hazelnuts
- 3 Tbsp of coconut oil
- 2 cups almond flour
- 2 Tbsp of arrowroot tea
- 2 tsp ginger
- 1 Tbsp cocoa powder
- 1/2 cup grapefruit juice
- 1 orange peel from a half orange
- 1/2 tsp baking soda
- 1 pinch of salt

INSTRUCTIONS:
- Preheat oven to 360 F.
- Make arrowroot tea and let it cool.
- In a food processor blend the hazelnuts. Add the remaining ingredients and continue blending until mixed well. With your hands form cookies with the batter.
- Put the cookies on baking parchment paper, and bake for 30-35 minutes. When ready, remove the tray from the oven and let cool.
- Serve warm or cold.

NUTRITION: Calories 224.08 | Total Fats 20.17g | Net Carbs: 8.06g | Protein 6.36g | Fiber 3.25 g)

88. Tartar Zero-Belly Cookies

Total Time: 35 MIN| Serve: 8)

INGREDIENTS:
- 3 eggs
- 1/8 tsp cream of tartar
- 1/3 cup cream cheese
- 1/8 tsp salt
- Some oil for greasing

INSTRUCTIONS:
- Preheat oven to 300 F.
- Line the cookie sheet with parchment paper and grease with some oil.
- Separate eggs from the egg yolks. Set both in different mixing bowls.
- With an electric hand mixer, start beating the egg whites until super bubbly. Add in cream of tartar and beat until stiff peaks form.
- In the egg yolk bowl, add in cream cheese and some salt. Beat until the egg yolks are pale yellow.
- Merge the egg whites into the cream cheese mixture. Stir well.
- Make cookies and place on the cookie sheet.
- Bake for about 30-40 minutes. When ready, let them cool on a wire rack and serve.

NUTRITION: Calories 59.99 | Total Fats 5.09g | Net Carbs: 0.56g | Protein 2.93g)

89. Wild Strawberries Ice Cream

Total Time: 5 MIN| Serve: 4

INGREDIENTS:
- 1/2 cup wild strawberries
- 1/3 cup cream cheese
- 1 cup heavy cream
- 1 Tbsp lemon juice
- 1 tsp pure vanilla extract
- 1/3 cup of your favorite sweetener
- Ice cubes

INSTRUCTIONS:
- Place all ingredients in a blender. Blend until all incorporate well.
- Refrigerate for 2-3 hour before serving.

NUTRITION: Calories 176.43 | Total Fats 17.69g | Net Carbs: 3.37g | Protein 1.9g | Fiber 0.39g)

90. Mini Lemon Cheesecakes

Total Time: 5 MIN | Serve: 6

INGREDIENTS:
- 1 tbsp lemon zest, grated
- 1 tsp lemon juice
- ½ tsp stevia powder or (Truvia)
- 1/4 cup coconut oil, softened
- 4 tbsp unsalted butter, softened
- 4 ounces cream cheese (heavy cream)

INSTRUCTIONS:
- Blend all ingredients together with a hand mixer or blender until smooth and creamy.
- Prepare a cupcake or muffin tin with 6 paper liners.
- Pour mixture into prepared tin and place in freezer for 2-3 hours or until firm.
- Sprinkle cups with additional lemon zest. Or try using chopped nuts or shredded, unsweetened coconut.

NUTRITION: Calories 213 | Total Fats 23g | Net Carbs: 0.7g | Protein 1.5g | Fiber: 0.1 g)

91. Fudgy Peanut Butter Squares

Total Time: 10 MIN| Serve: 12

INGREDIENTS:
- 1 cup all natural creamy peanut butter
- 1 cup coconut oil
- 1/4 cup unsweetened vanilla almond milk
- a pinch of coarse sea salt
- 1 tsp vanilla extract
- 2 tsp liquid stevia (optional)

INSTRUCTIONS:
- In a microwave-safe bowl, soften the peanut butter and coconut oil together. (About 1 minute on med-low heat.)
- Combine the softened peanut butter and coconut oil with the remaining ingredients into a blender or food processor.
- Blend until thoroughly combined.
- Pour into a 9X4" loaf pan that has been lined with parchment paper.
- Refrigerate until set. About 2 hours.
- Enjoy.

NUTRITION: Calories 292 | Total Fats 28.9g | Net Carbs: 4.1g | Protein 6g | Fiber 1.4g)

92. Lemon Squares & Coconut Cream

Total Time: 1 HR 5 MIN| Serve: 8)

INGREDIENTS:
BASE:
- 3/4 cup coconut flakes
- 2 Tbsp coconut oil
- 1 Tbsp ground almonds

CREAM:
- 5 eggs
- 1/2 lemon juice
- 1 Tbsp coconut flour
- 1/2 cup Stevia sweetener

INSTRUCTIONS:
FOR THE BASE
- Preheat oven to 360 F.
- In a bowl put all base ingredients and with clean hands mix everything well until soft.
- With coconut oil grease a rectangle oven dish. Pour dough into a baking pan. Bake for 15 minutes until golden brown. Set aside to cool.

FOR THE CREAM
- In a bowl or blender, whisk together: eggs, lemon juice, coconut flour, and sweetener. Pour over the baked caked evenly.
- Put the pan in the oven and bake 20 minutes more.
- When ready refrigerate for at least 6 hours. Cut into cubes and serve.

NUTRITION: Calories 129 | Total Fats 15g | Net Carbs: 1.4g | Protein 5g | Fiber 2.25g)

93. Rich Almond Butter Cake & Chocolate Sauce

Total Time: 10 MIN| Serve: 12

INGREDIENTS:
- 1 cup almond butter or soaked almonds
- 1/4 cup almond milk, unsweetened
- 1 cup coconut oil
- 2 tsp liquid Stevia sweetener to taste

TOPPING: CHOCOLATE SAUCE
- 4 Tbsp cocoa powder, unsweetened
- 2 Tbsp almond butter
- 2 Tbsp Stevia sweetener

INSTRUCTIONS:
- Melt the coconut oil in room temperature.
- Add all ingredients in a bowl and blend well until combined.
- Pour the almond butter mixture into a parchment lined platter.
- Place in refrigerator for 3 hours.
- In a bowl, whisk all topping ingredients together. Pour over the almond cake after it's been set. Cut into cubes and serve.

NUTRITION: Calories 273 | Total Fats 23.3g | Net Carbs: 2.4g | Protein 5.8g | Fiber 2g)

94. Peanut Butter Cake Covered in Chocolate Sauce

Total Time: 10 MIN | Serve: 12

INGREDIENTS:
- 1 cup peanut butter
- 1/4 cup almond milk, unsweetened
- 1 cup coconut oil
- 2 tsp liquid Stevia sweetener to taste

TOPPING: CHOCOLATE SAUCE
- 2 Tbsp coconut oil, melted
- 4 Tbsp cocoa powder, unsweetened
- 2 Tbsp Stevia sweetener

INSTRUCTIONS:
- In a microwave bowl mix coconut oil and peanut butter; melt in a microwave for 1-2 minutes.
- Add this mixture to your blender; add in the rest of the ingredients and blend well until combined.
- Pour the peanut mixture into a parchment lined loaf pan or platter.
- Refrigerate for about 3 hours; the longer, the better.
- In a bowl, whisk all topping ingredients together. Pour over the peanut candy after it's been set. Cut into cubes and serve.

NUTRITION: Calories 273 | Total Fats 27g | Net Carbs: 2.4g | Protein 6g | Fiber 2g)

SMOOTHIES

95.Green Coconut Smoothie

Total Time: 10 MIN| Serve: 2

INGREDIENTS:
- 1 cup coconut milk
- 1 green apple, cored and chopped
- 1 cup spinach
- 1 cucumber
- 2 Tbsp shaved coconut
- 1/2 cup water
- Ice cubes (if needed)

INSTRUCTIONS:
- Put all ingredients and ice in a blender; pulse until smooth.
- Serve immediately.

NUTRITION: Calories 216.57 | Total Fats 16.56g | Net Carbs: 8.79g | Protein 2.88g | Fiber: 4g)

96. Green Devil Smoothie

Total Time: 10 MIN | Serve: 2

INGREDIENTS:
- 3 cup kale, fresh
- 1/2 cup coconut yogurt
- 1/2 cup broccoli, florets
- 2 celery stalk, chopped
- 2 cup water
- 1 Tbsp lemon juice
- Ice cubes (if needed)

INSTRUCTIONS:
- Blend all ingredients together until smooth and slightly frothy.

NUTRITION: Calories 117.09 | Total Fats 4.98g | Net Carbs: 1.89g | Protein 4.09g | Fiber 6.18g)

97. Green Dream Zero-Belly Smoothie

Total Time: 10 MIN| Serve: 4

INGREDIENTS:
- 1 cup raw cucumber, peeled and sliced
- 4 cups water
- 1 cup romaine lettuce
- 1 cup Haas avocado
- 2 Tbsp fresh basil
- Sweetener of your choice (optional)
- Handful of walnuts
- 2 Tbsp fresh parsley
- 1 Tbsp fresh ginger grated
- Ice cubes (optional)

INSTRUCTIONS:
- In a blender, combine all of the ingredients and pulse until smooth.
- Add ice if used. Serve cold.

NUTRITION: Calories 50.62| Total Fats 3.89g | Net Carbs: 1.07g | Protein 1.1g | Fiber 2.44g)

98. Zero-Belly Celery and Nut Smoothie

Total Time: 10 MIN| Serve: 2

INGREDIENTS:
- 2 celery stem
- 1 cup spinach leaves, roughly chopped
- 1/2 cup pistachio nuts (unsalted)
- 1/2 avocado, chopped
- 1/2 cup lime, juice
- 1 Tbsp Hemp seeds
- 1 Tbsp almonds, soaked
- 1 cup coconut water
- Ice cubes (optional)

INSTRUCTIONS:
- Add all ingredients in a blender with a few ice cubes and blend until smooth.

NUTRITION: Calories 349.55 | Total Fats 17.88g | Net Carbs: 5.01g | Protein 11.08g | Fiber 9.8g)

99. Lime Peppermint Smoothie

Total Time: 5 MIN| Serve: 4

INGREDIENTS:
- 1/4 cup fresh mint leaves
- 1/4 cup lime juice
- 1/2 cup cucumber, chopped
- 1 Tbsp fresh basil leaves, chopped
- 1 tsp chia seed (optional)
- Handful of chia seeds
- 3 tsp zest of limes
- Sweetener of your choice to taste
- 1 cup water, divided
- Ice as needed

INSTRUCTIONS:
- Place all ingredients in a blender or food processor. Pulse until smooth well.
- Fill glasses with ice, pour the limeade into each glass, and enjoy.

NUTRITION: Calories 28.11 | Total Fats 1.16g | Net Carbs: 0.75g | Protein 0.84g | Fiber 1.98g)

100. Red Grapefruit Kale Smoothies

Total Time: 10 MIN| Serve: 4

INGREDIENTS:
- 2 cups cantaloupe
- 1/4 cup fresh strawberries
- 8 oz coconut yogurt
- 2 cups kale leaves, chopped
- 2 Tbsp sweetener of your taste
- 1 Ice as needed
- 1 cup water

INSTRUCTIONS:
- Clean the grapefruit and remove the seeds.
- Combine all ingredients in an electric blender and whirl until smooth. Add ice if used and serve.

NUTRITION: Calories 260.74 | Total Fats 11.57g | Net Carbs: 2.96g | Protein 4.42g | Fiber 7.23g)

CONCLUSION

As we conclude this transformative journey, we hope that the Zero Belly Cookbook has inspired you to embrace a nourishing and balanced approach to eating. The recipes and principles shared in this cookbook are designed to help you achieve a healthier body and a happier, more energetic life.

With the Zero Belly Cookbook, you have the tools to make positive changes in your eating habits. Each recipe is carefully crafted to provide you with the nutrients you need while supporting your weight loss and overall health goals. By embracing the Zero Belly approach, you're not just adopting a short-term diet, but rather a long-term lifestyle that promotes sustainable health and well-being.

So, as you continue on your path to a healthier you, let the Zero Belly Cookbook be your trusted companion, providing you with nourishing recipes, helpful tips, and a sense of empowerment. Embrace the power of wholesome ingredients, mindful eating, and a balanced approach to nutrition. Each meal you prepare from this cookbook is an opportunity to nourish your body and make choices that support your overall well-being.

May your kitchen be filled with the aromas of nourishing ingredients, the joy of cooking, and the satisfaction of nourishing your body with delicious meals. Cheers to a healthier you and a life of vitality and wellness!

www.ingramcontent.com/pod-product-compliance
Lightning Source LLC
LaVergne TN
LVHW021700060526
838200LV00050B/2446